BENDING THE RULES

BENDING THE RULES

FASHION BEYOND THE BINARY

CAMILLE BENDA

with Gwyn Conaway

PA PRESS

PRINCETON ARCHITECTURAL PRESS · NEW YORK

Published by
Princeton Architectural Press
A division of Chronicle Books LLC
70 West 36th Street
New York, NY 10018
papress.com

Editor: Jennifer N. Thompson
Designer: Natalie Snodgrass

Library of Congress Cataloging-in-Publication Data
Names: Benda, Camille author | Conaway, Gwyn author
Title: Bending the rules : fashion beyond the binary /
    Camille Benda with Gwyn Conaway.
Description: First edition. | New York, NY : Princeton
    Architectural Press, 2026. | Includes bibliographical
    references. | Summary: "Text, graphics, timelines,
    and photography exploring identity and gender through
    fashion and dress"—Provided by publisher.
Identifiers: LCCN 2025016865 | ISBN 9781797227610
    hardcover | ISBN 9781797227627 ebook
Subjects: LCSH: Sexual minorities—Clothing | Clothing and
    dress—Social aspects | Sexual minorities—Identity
Classification: LCC GT1725 .B46 2026 | DDC 391.0081—
    dc23/eng/20250606
LC record available at https://lccn.loc.gov/2025016865

CONTENTS

FOREWORD

Gender and attire have always been intimately connected. In our far-from-equal present day, gender-expansive people often queer gendered fashion norms as expressions of their gender identities or as visual critiques of norms and stereotypes. Frequently, nonbinary people adopt forms of dress that are not the norm for their assigned gender at birth to express their gender. Thus, *Queer Eye* star Jonathan Van Ness favors dresses and skirts, while Canadian British comedian Mae Martin hits the red carpet in tuxedos. Other forms of resistance to gendered fashion rules range from eschewing marks of gender altogether through unisex styles to combining elements marked as gendered into riotous androgynous mashups.

Consider the "skant," a minidress-shorts combo introduced on the pilot episode of *Star Trek: The Next Generation* and worn by both men and women. The costume designer for the series, William Ware Theiss, developed the skant to represent the gender equality of the future. However, the skant was short-lived. No main characters wore it after the pilot episode, more women wore it than men, and it was gone by season 2. The skant was intended to be emancipatory, but emancipation is never easy.

While the "rules" for gendered attire vary over time and place, they are often strictly enforced, with stigma attached to violating them. Further, norms for gender expression in attire tend to be highly binaristic. Among gender roles—which can include not only attire but forms of work, leisure activities, religious roles, and so on—dress and fashion are among the most closely policed. In some contexts, breaking the rules is dangerous. People who violate norms of gendered attire risk mockery, harassment, or violence. It takes courage to queer fashion! But in aggregate, those acts of courage expand the possibilities for people of all genders. Women today can wear trousers to work because women of the last century had the courage to break the rules. Paradoxically, the strictness of the gendered attire rule book invites challenge and resistance more than lax norms would. Such challenges range from the playful to the revolutionary. If enough of us break today's fashion rules, we can hope for a future in which, for more than just the select few of us, fashion provides a way to joyfully express one's gender rather than a shroud to conceal it.

—Shannon Dea, December 2024, Dean of arts, professor, philosophy and classics, University of Regina

INTRODUCTION
∞ (INFINITY)

This is a book of many voices—a workbook, a scrapbook, a collection of short passages woven around images. The images in this book lead the way; the text follows as more than 170 illustrations, custom 3D renderings, photographs, artworks, sketches, digital drawings, self-portraits, magazine covers, iPhone snapshots, and paintings wind their way across geography and time. Images are grouped by themes and juxtaposed with each other to tell a short story, highlight a phenomenon, or share a quick dip into fashion history. Using something we all have in common—the clothing we wear—to find commonalities, points of connection and mutual understanding in our image-saturated, fast-paced global world is an overarching theme of this book.

Clothes show us what language cannot tell us. Dress, adornment, accessories, hair, makeup, footwear, and textiles are the nonverbal, visual tools that we use to imagine ourselves when language, vocabulary, written texts, and societal rules are expanding, changing and realigning. Fashion helps us see beyond the binary, allowing us to construct our identities one item of clothing at a time. Language and clothing intertwine, from pronouns to fashion terms, across the globe and throughout history. If a culture has traditionally held space for the language of expansive gender identity, then that identity was important to that culture from the beginning. If that language is missing, individuals must create space for it, with both their bodies and their words. People's words matter, and their descriptions of themselves are important. I quote noteworthy passages directly and feature multiple interviews so individuals can speak for themselves.

Throughout the book, cultural experts, historians across the world, and firsthand accounts speak directly to the reader. The digital illustrations in each chapter bring to life underrepresented historical figures; rare archival images provide a glimpse into bygone times; and surviving examples of antique fashion and ancient garments show how humans are connected across millennia through dress. The cultural history of clothes tells us so much about the future, so past and present examples of rule-bending fashions are interspersed with inspiration from artists and designers who are actively visioning what's coming next.

Both the introduction and afterword are subtitled "Infinity" because the combination of fashion, dress, accessories, hair, makeup, gender identity, self-expression, and the body are infinite. Threads of childhood memories are woven throughout the book;

childhood is where our gendered ideas first develop, and those ideas might need to be shed later in life to get beyond the binary. Getting "beyond the binary" means first deeply understanding it and why its power has such a hold on Western culture, since gender expansiveness has been with us for at least five thousand years. Western fashion depends on the binary and going beyond that requires innovation and creative thinking.

Six themes frame the exploration of the binary and beyond, and why binary fashion is actually the newest development in dress history, not the default. First, the idea of 0 (Neutrality) looks at many current and past cultures that make or made space for gender-expansive language and fashion. Closely linked is the idea of X (Unisex), which reveals the gendered body more than it unifies it. The chapter on 0/1 (Binary) fashion looks at not only binary rituals and ceremonies like proms and weddings but also how trousers and skirts ended up on opposing sides of the Western fashion divide. After 0/1, the numbers I, II, and III represent the linked ideas of Singular identities, focusing on hypermasculine and hyperfeminine presentation and how they can be subverted; Duality, how individuals across time have held opposing binaries in one body and used a dual nature for self-expression; and Triad, the power of three, exploring Two-Spirit, third-gender, and gender-expansive people.

The power of three also plays a part in the introduction and afterword, each of which includes three individuals who are living and creating beyond the binary. They are featured outside the six themes because all of them exemplify the overarching ideas of the book. To start, Qween Jean outwardly shares her joyous self-expression with the world through her everyday life. Michael Sylvan Robinson uses textile arts to amplify queer voices, and Charles Fréger preserves cultural traditions through his photography but simultaneously questions their place in modern society.

QWEEN JEAN

For costume designer and queer activist Qween Jean, clothes are deeply linked to her personal identity as well as her artistic practice. Costume designers deeply immerse themselves in research to distill and reflect it back to the directors, producers, actors, and creative team on any given project, whether it's modern, historical, or fantasy. For Qween Jean, life is not only about the costumes but also about

OPPOSITE
Costume designer Qween Jean's passion for clothes is deeply personal. Cover, *American Theatre*, 2023.

AMERICAN THEATRE

FALL 2023   VOL 40, NO. 1   THEATRE COMMUNICATIONS GROUP

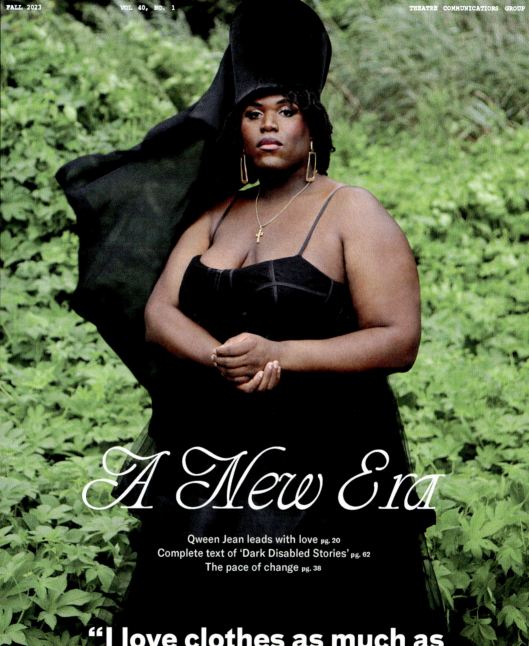

A New Era

Qween Jean leads with love pg. 20
Complete text of 'Dark Disabled Stories' pg. 62
The pace of change pg. 38

"I love clothes as much as I love my freedom. My clothes are an extension of myself."

—Qween Jean

her personal everyday fashion choices. Her choices are not without risk, but they emit a sense of joy and celebration.

Qween Jean balances her costume design practice with work for fashion houses and as a mentor for youth activism. As a gender-nonconforming Black woman, Qween feels, "We should always disrupt the gender binary narrative," and notes that geography can affect people's perception of her appearance. In New York, Qween is at home on the streets, but in Texas, "When I show up in a Walmart," she says, "people go crazy." Qween's personal appearance was triggering to some at her high school job at Big K Tobacco in South Florida, where she grew up. Patrons would report her to customer service for wearing makeup. Such encounters caused her to ask the question, "What does it mean to look decent?"

The question "What does it mean to look…" permeates the book.

MICHAEL SYLVAN ROBINSON

Genderqueer fiber artist, activist, and arts educator Michael Sylvan Robinson produces work that encompasses the infinite. Using a dizzying array of textiles, trims, sequins, custom-printed materials, vintage fabrics, offcuts, and scraps, they create exquisite handworked pieces that highlight the power of storytelling through garments. In speaking with Robinson, they shared how "queer people want ancestors." Robinson says that fashion and identity cannot be separated. It's the story of a coat, or a robe, or a mantle—the words and how a garment is gendered may change, but the garment stays the same.

In the following interview, Robinson describes their process in creating the sensational "coat of many colors" for theater producer Jordan Roth.[2]

Benda: How did the commission to create Jordan Roth's 2021 Met Gala coat come about?

Robinson: I had created a garment that I called "Priestessing the Work of Healing." It was like a 1960s kite gown—very personal with lots of text work on it—and it ended up being photographed by Guinevere van Seenus for *Vogue Germany*. Michael Philouze, who is the men's editor for *Vogue* magazine, was the stylist for that shoot. Six weeks later, I get this email from Michael: We'd like you to consider making a garment for Jordan Roth. I literally was like, oh, come on!

OPPOSITE
Detail of Michael Sylvan Robinson's design for Jordan Roth's Met Gala look, 2021.

I think the reason why I got picked, in some ways, was this idea of gender expression that we shared and were able to explore together.

Benda: What was your process in working with Jordan?

Robinson: Jordan came to see me at my studio, and we looked at a piece I'd made entitled "Love Letter to Queer Descendants." It featured embellished peacock imagery as an expression of both pride and protection; some of our initial conversation inspired the use of peacock imagery in the Met Gala garment. The garment itself has a real peacock-tail quality: the coat can fold in on itself. When the coat turns, pieces that are on opposite sides can end up next to each other. It's a kaleidoscope or mirror ball effect. Text that wasn't visible is revealed. In some way, could that be a metaphor for gender identity? Shouldn't we all just be allowed to expand and contract as needed?

Jordan's initial intention for the Met Gala design was to have embroidered and beaded poetic phrases from his own writing across the surface of the garment. Michael responded to this prompt from Roth: "Identity is a construction. So, too, is a garment. Some are created by the wearers themselves. Some are projected on the wearers by others. Identity is in a constant state of making and unmaking, of weaving and unraveling. It's a dance of making and unmaking and remaking itself, creating a sense that it is being made and unmade as it is being worn. Am I weaving and unraveling it? Is it weaving and unraveling itself? Yes."

LEFT
Michael Sylvan Robinson's "Coat of Many Colors" for the "Identity Is…" installation at the Museum of Arts and Design in 2024.

RIGHT
Michael Sylvan Robinson with the "Coat of Many Colors," which gazes back at the viewer with its many eye motifs.

BENDING THE RULES: FASHION BEYOND THE BINARY

Benda: The coat uses repeated symbols like eyes, women's faces, flowers, and natural motifs. What do these symbols mean to you?

Robinson: One of the things that Jordan and I talked about is that I come from a queer activist background, and I use decorative work—all the beading, all the sequins, all the color, and that beautiful energy of the handwork and the use of eye motifs as recurring symbols of protection—as a kind of maximalist way of pushing beyond, as a way of queering. I went back to the Met and took photos of some of my favorite gendered sculptures and then queered them in my way onto Jordan's garment.

In my work there's always this kind of queering of art history that I continue to come back to. As a young person growing up in Europe, I was very inspired by the ancient world. I had a lot of exposure to museums, and things from ancient times still fascinate me today. We look back at history and we want to put our own layers on it. This is especially true for queer people, whose identities have been erased, persecuted, and manipulated.

CHARLES FRÉGER

In a series of chats with photographer Charles Fréger, he revealed much about the creation of identity—of a nation, a person, a costume, and folk dress. Fréger travels the world, beautifully photographing the brilliant colors, textures, and patterns of global dress and revealing the endless human capacity to create tradition and ceremony.

Fréger crisscrossed rural Japan from 2013 to 2015, photographing ritual costumes in natural settings, following figures including yōkai, oni, tengu, and kappa (ghosts, monsters, ogres, and goblins) through a real and imagined landscape. The following two photographs of New Year's ceremonies from his *Yokainoshima* series show the traditional dress and overt sexual symbols of the tanokami and tanokami yome (rice paddy gods), who use their sticks as talismans to ensure a bountiful harvest. Fréger calls this series part of his "personal cartography," which maps through earthly and otherworldly lands at the same time.[3] He believes that social media is changing the makeup of these earthly lands. As the same homogenized images are shared by everyone, they dilute what was unique and magical about traditional dress, national identity, and what cultures hold dear.

Yokainoshima Portrait, 2013–2015.
Wearing traditional festival dress, this
female figure carries a "vagina stick."

Yokainoshima Portrait, 2013–2015.
This figure, also in traditional festival
dress, carries a "penis stick."

(NEUTRALITY)

"Comfort ≠ peace. Sometimes, seeking peace requires making people uncomfortable."

—Kodo Nishimura, artist and Buddhist monk

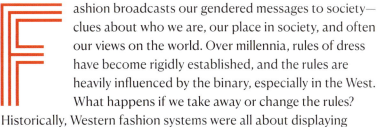

ashion broadcasts our gendered messages to society—clues about who we are, our place in society, and often our views on the world. Over millennia, rules of dress have become rigidly established, and the rules are heavily influenced by the binary, especially in the West. What happens if we take away or change the rules? Historically, Western fashion systems were all about displaying gender, but this book follows trailblazers who are dismantling rigid rules with a more fluid remix of garments as genderfluid, genderless, and gender-inclusive individuals take the traditional fashion toolbox and rebuild it in their unique image. Nonbinary activists like Alok Vaid-Menon choose clothes according to mood, occasion, and taste rather than rigid binary fashion rules.

The binary doesn't need to be the starting point for fashion and dress. Individual clothing pieces don't have gender, but have gender attributed to them, and even that changes across geography, language, and time. The basis of all ancient Greek dress was the chiton (χιτών), a T-shaped tunic worn by all genders (with different layers and variations). Similarly, the Hebrew kethoneth (כְּתֹנֶת) was the most elemental body covering for everyone. By the time the ancient Romans adopted the garment, the name changed and the words were genderized in Latin: *tunic* for men or *tunica* for women. When fashions change, then the rules, language, and customs that surround the clothes change too.

Emilia Bergoglio, contributor to the Seamwork website, founded by Sarai Mitnik, inspires readers with their nonbinary style and exploration of non-gendered sewing, highlighting the natural contradiction between biological body shape and gender presentation in dressmaking and tailoring practices. Bergoglio notes that not just wearing clothes but also creating them starts from a gendered patternmaking practice and spreads widely across ready-to-wear and high fashion.

Chloe Chapin, dress historian and author, analyzes this practice in discussing the gender binary:

> When you talk about contemporary fashion, it is gendered at every stage of the production process. It's gendered in the patterning, it's gendered in the sizing, it's gendered in the runway, it's gendered in the department store floor. It's gendered at the marketing. It's gendered in the mannequins who wear it.[1]

This chapter's exploration of gender neutrality in fashion starts with undergarments. For binary individuals, traditional undergarments can be affirming. For trans people, they can be dysphoric or euphoric depending on how they support their gender identity. The layers closest to our skin can be highly genderized or completely neutral, but for a long time there were only gendered options. The choice is up to us, our culture, and our preferences. Gender-inclusive brand Urbody, one of the pioneers of neutral undergarments, is known for meeting customers' needs across the gender identity spectrum.

Some couture brands and experimental designers are creating gender-neutral and gender-inclusive fashion that steps out of the regular world and moves into the conceptual one. Bernhard Willhelm, Rick Owens, Issey Miyake, Rei Kawakubo, and Yohji Yamamoto wrestle with complex ideas beyond the binary. This chapter also examines fashion subcultures like Lolita dressing and Japanese "herbivore men" and "carnivore women" that question gendered clothing.

Moving on from fashion, this chapter shows how certain works of literature and film explore the creation of self. Image creation in children's dress and gender neutrality (and the neutralizing of gender) in portraiture and books reflect invented conceptions of virtue that society layers onto youngsters and women. Virginia Woolf's gender-bending literary character Orlando shows us how cinematic magic happens as they switch from male to female bodies across time and space in Sally Potter's film adaptation. Potter herself wrote a custom description for this book of how she brought Woolf's literary work to screen.

Then, from the conceptual into the virtual, we enter worlds where video games and alternate universes let adult players try on any identity they want through avatars, and films like *The Fifth Element* and *Minority Report* envision future neutrality.

Finally, we review early European artists who took on the challenge of portraying angels, thought to be gender neutral, with no human body in their earthly form, while the primitive science of alchemy explored androgyny. Spirituality and neutrality are linked as a look at Buddhist robes wraps up the chapter.

OPPOSITE
Weaver Jon Riis uses the traditional art of tapestry to explore human history through rich color, detailed patterns, and multilayered beading. Woven silk kimono with coral beads, 2005.

FLESH
KIMONO

This intricately woven kimono displaying muscles and connective tissue is an analogy of how we are all the same underneath our skin before gender identity is layered on us.

"The red tapestry in a kimono shape represents man's muscle. Garments cover parts of the human body and provide an expression of personal taste and style. In contrast, this work discloses that humans have an internal structure in common. For the artist, what's inside one man is not very different from all other men."[2]

URBODY
FOR EVERY BODY

Anna Graham and Mere Abrams, founders of gender-affirming underwear and activewear line Urbody, were inspired by personal experience to bring innovation to the undergarment market. All types of people on the gender spectrum seek out Urbody for their health-conscious compression garments, gaffs, and packing underwear. I chatted with Graham about why and how the line began.

Benda: Why does Urbody focus on creating gender-affirming undergarments, and how did the brand spring to life?

Graham: Traditional underwear, like much of the fashion industry, has been built around binary ideas of bodies and self-expression. If you are in a body that does not match your gender identity, the right clothes and underwear can make you feel affirmed. Urbody underwear is fluid; customers can shop across categories and avoid being boxed in. We aim to create a space where self-expression and exploration are not only possible but encouraged.

Benda: Gender identity is often a progression, and Urbody is creating an intermediate space for people to experiment with who they are. How did you pinpoint your brand focus?

Graham: We like to say we're a brand for the human being! Our focus has always been on creating clothing for all people regardless of where they are in their journey. At Urbody, we often hear from our customers who feel a newfound sense of euphoria and freedom when they wear our pieces, something they haven't experienced before. We're proud to offer garments that allow individuals to express their true selves, helping them feel seen and celebrated in what they wear.

Benda: Urbody started by fostering strong relationships with the communities it serves. How do you continue that connection?

Graham: Our connection to the community is foundational. When it comes to model casting, we look directly to our community, often through social media. We actively seek out a variety of body types, ethnicities, and gender expressions—many of our models return for multiple campaigns, and we've built strong relationships over time. We also launched the Fully Human Giveback Program alongside Urbody, which allows us to support and uplift queer and trans artists. This year, we're excited to support geologist and singer-songwriter Katie Castagno.

OPPOSITE
This 2024 campaign celebrates models from the Urbody community, so that all customers can see someone who reflects their own experience in the advertising.

BEEFCAKE
SWIMWEAR FOR THE SPECTRUM

Another fashion necessity (but something no one ever wants to shop for) is a good bathing suit. Mel Brittner Wells, founder of Beefcake Swimwear, rewrote the rules when she made a 1920s-inspired swimsuit for a friend who couldn't find anything off the rack that was stylish and nicely fitted. Wells hoped there might be a small, niche market for the design, but knew it was a tough sell. A few years later, the suits were shipping around the world to all kinds of body types, ages, and gender expressions. The demand for joyous, gender-nonconforming swimwear was out there, waiting.

"While our swimsuits are gender neutral, the people wearing them don't have to be. The whole concept it that our swimwear can be comfortable and fun for anyone, across the gender spectrum."[3]

Beefcake Swimwear's 2024 photoshoot in a
Montana locker room features neutral suits
on models across the gender spectrum.

GENDERFUL

"I just wanted to be hot," said queer music icon Troye Sivan when asked why he chose "genderful" brand Altu for his 2021 Met Gala Parade of Departures look. The idea of "hot" used to be divided into male and female, and what was hot for each biological gender. Now it can be for everyone, and hot doesn't have to be attached to gender attributes, but to individual fashion choices.

"Genderful" is how Joseph Altuzarra describes his diffusion line, Altu, and it's definitely not unisex, he says. Altuzarra thinks of Altu as "almost more like a cultural project, it sort of exists outside of fashion."[4] Nicole Phelps at *Vogue* quotes Altuzarra and notes how an explosion of brands began deconstructing the gender binary:

> "I'm aware for sure that I'm not the first person to explore this," Altuzarra says. "What's interesting about what we're doing is that we're trying to operate outside of the binary. I didn't want to design men's clothes for women," or vice versa. Retailers and e-tailers have some work to do to catch up; toggling between men and women is the first click most sites ask us to make.[5]

A deep scoop neck, side cutouts, slinky fabric, and body-hugging columnar design both reveal and conceal in this 2021 snap of Troye Sivan leaving The Mark Hotel in New York City.

BENDING THE RULES: FASHION BEYOND THE BINARY

HARDER AND STRANGER

esides Altu, only a handful of haute couture and ready-to-wear brands tackle a strong silhouette that fits multiple genders. Comb through thousands of runway photos, and almost none feature models of different genders wearing the same garment. Many designers create essential staples of a modern urban ward-robe: long T-shirt, a neutral simple pant, a high-top sneaker. But to create an experi-mental, structured, body-hugging piece for more than one gender identity—like the ones from Los Angeles native Rick Owens's Spring/Summer 2022 collection in Paris—is remarkable. On pages 30 and 31, the two black dresses with geometric, structured bodices are not identical but use the same

corseted torso shape to create an anchor for variations in skirt length, accessories, boots, and hair. Although Owens's designs feel futuristic at first glance, the ancient world, early textiles, classical Greek draping, and early medieval tailoring echo throughout his collections. This alchemy of ancient and futuristic is why he is described in the fashion press as a visionary, iconoclast, rebel, and, most dramatically, "The Lord of Darkness."[6] On the runway, Owens proposes that the binary doesn't have to be the starting point for dressing the body.

"I'm not quite sure why gender fluidity gained so much traction recently, because it's been done. It's been done harder and stranger."[7]

"There is something monstrous about his gothic garments...When people wear them head to toe, as Owens's most enthusiastic followers frequently do, they don't look human. They look other."[8]

Paris Fashion Week
Look No. 0019,
Ready to Wear Spring/
Summer 2022. In
Rick Owens's creative
universe, body types,
hair, and makeup are
inseparable from the
clothes.

Casting beautifully unique and unconventional models, actors, and musicians for the runway is part of Rick Owens's aesthetic vision. Paris Fashion Week Look No. 0006, Ready to Wear Spring/Summer 2022.

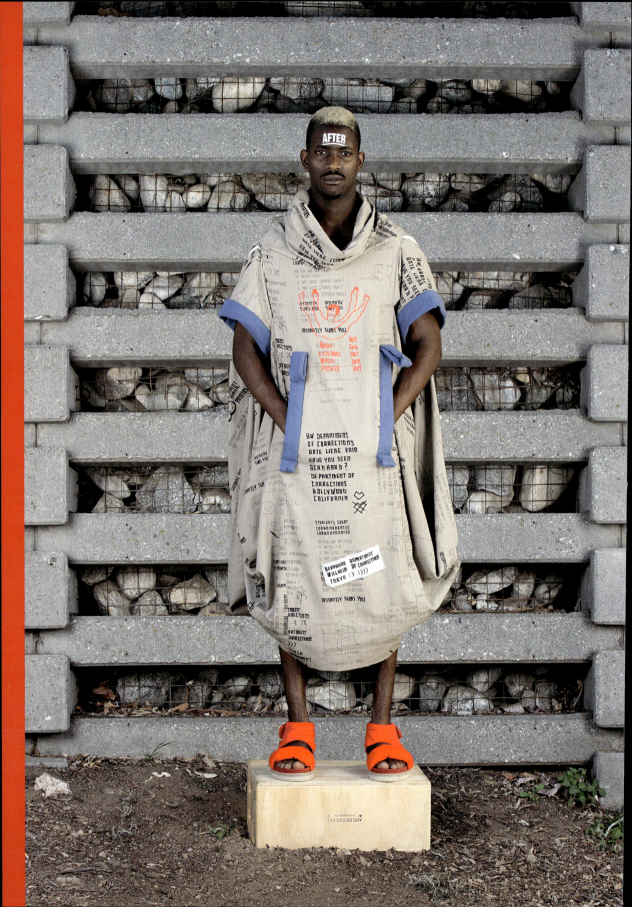

BERNHARD WILLHELM
THE MAGIC POTATO SMOCK

German fashion designer Bernhard Willhelm explores similar territory in a very different way. An all-encompassing garment, like this whimsical piece from his collection, is gender inclusive to the core. It envelops the wearer like a cocoon and leaves space for personal expression through hair, makeup, shoes, and accessories. It is covered with custom illustrations and slogans like "body external magic potato" and "have you seen Bernhard?," which makes each piece unique and directly engages the wearer and viewer. In an exchange of messages over Instagram, Willhelm described the garment: "It's an egg-shaped beige toga with padded asymmetric azure pockets in Japanese cotton. The sandals have a padded, raw-edge upper with a Velcro strap in red velvet from Japan with a caoutchouc [natural rubber] sole handmade in Italy. The TYPO print design of the toga is made by German artist Carsten Fock, who also created the letter type and logo for [my brand]. We have collaborated for thirty years."[9]

Willhelm entertains the eye with the clothes he designs, and sometimes his runway shows are fully choreographed experimental performances complete with custom sets and lighting. Strong colors, bold typefaces, vibrant textile patterns, graphic fabric treatments, experimental materials, and traditional German folk dress, headwear, and masks all feature in the clothes he designs. Because he creates loose drop-crotch trousers, oversized hoodies, draped and twisted jersey dresses, voluminous tunics, and pleated, adjustable skirts, his fashions fit a wide range of bodies. His exhibitions in Belgium, Germany, and the United States use his clothes like gender-bending art pieces set around a museum in playful vignettes—anonymous mannequins with their heads stuck in a TV, for example, or wearing fishnet tights and pink-soled tennis shoes while fixing a smashed car.

OPPOSITE
Bernhard Willhelm's fashion vision for this Fall/Winter 2016 shoot in Altadena, CA, featured Jamal Berotte, Willhelm's favorite Los Angeles–based model, who was photographed by Daniele Trese.

JAPANESE DESIGNERS

In late-1960s Japan, a unique blossoming of three fashion designers took the human form as a starting point for questioning how fashion functions. They changed the trajectory of twentieth-century fashion and continue to challenge how we see clothing, gender identity, and the body in the twenty-first century.

In 1969 Rei Kawakubo started Comme des Garçons, a womenswear house with a French name meaning "Like the Boys." Adding menswear in 1978, Kawakubo exploded the boundaries of the body with conceptual clothing that subverted gender norms. A year later, Issey Miyake founded his design practice and in 1981 added the genderless, ageless Plantation line. He followed with Pleats Please and Homme Plissé, which used the traditional craft of pleating to envelop the body in volume and form. Yohji Yamamoto began designing in 1972 and rounded out the trio of visionaries who would shape Japanese fashion forever.

Rei Kawakubo uses sculptural shapes to disrupt the surface of the body, creating architectural forms that welcome gender experimentation. Starting with a specific textile, an image, or an inspiring work of art, she develops rules and restrictions that produce a narrow design framework. Looking back at her runway shows from the 1990s, we can see the first glimmers of current trends (sheer, breast-revealing womenswear, for instance) that have taken twenty-five years to develop. Kawakubo is fearless; dipping into historical shapes while exploring new ones, her ideas rival any Elizabethan corset and butterfly ruff combination.

ISSEY MIYAKE

YOHJI YAMAMOTO

Issey Miyake's visionary patternmaking and strategic pleating transform when draped on the body. Effortless looking but technically challenging, his pieces free the human form rather than restrict it. Dancer Jawni Han relished wearing Pleats Please at a critical time in their life: "The fluidity of Miyake's garments leave me reassured that I could always obscure myself, a trans woman, and disengage from any fears of people scrutinizing my body....I might have certainties about my gender and body today, but that might change tomorrow—like Issey Miyake's pleats, my body does not have definite forms."[10]

Yohji Yamamoto mixes Victorian influences, experimental tailoring, and bespoke embellishments to create incredibly wearable pieces. His Fall/Winter 2024 menswear runway show featured female models walking the runway in men's pieces embellished with nonsensical sayings. The show included leather-laced corset tops layered with collared men's shirts, skirts, and softly draped coats. Other Yamamoto collections (he's been showing in Paris since 1981) have featured bright menswear pieces, sheer cardigans, and feathered gold brooches. Now eighty years old, Yamamoto casts models of a wide age and gender identity range who reflect the house's understanding of the fluidity and adaptability of clothes.

This 2024 digital collage of an "Herbivore Man" shows a more fluid masculine style: cozy cardigan, soft T-shirt, and casual jeans.

HERBIVORE MEN AND CARNIVORE WOMEN

Kawakubo, Miyake, and Yamamoto all played an indirect role in disrupting traditional Japanese culture as the battered nation opened to the West after WWII. While traditional male and female binary roles symbolized stability for Japanese families in the 1950s and '60s, the experimental fashion of these three designers gave Japanese youth an outlet for gender-expansive living in the 1970s and '80s. In the twenty-first century, Japanese people have swung away from the aggressive masculinity and docile femininity that had become symbolic of the abusive corporate culture that was common in post–WWII Japan, and the way they dress reflects this cultural change.

The contemporary "herbivore man" represents a rebellion against traditional macho, materialist perspectives and hyper-masculinity, choosing a passive, more neutral ground.[11] While standard-issue "salarymen"—business suit–wearing Japanese office workers (we'll see them later in the I Singular chapter)—are thought to embrace the commercialized relationship of buying a woman luxury goods or paying for their family's lifestyle rather than participating in it, herbivore men are characterized as being more interested in conserving resources and living a minimalist, simple life. Salarymen need luxury items such as

women's purses and perfumes to impress or "appease" a woman; herbivore men have an interest in male self-care, an interest traditionally associated with women. Buying for themselves, not others, herbivore men gravitate toward makeup, lingerie, cosmetic procedures, and home goods.

At the same time, so-called carnivore women are portrayed as being assertive on the dating scene and "hunting" for their partners with a business savvy one would have expected from a salaryman. Rather than wear camel coats, navy business suits, and gold watches, carnivore women tend toward Schiaparelli pink, manicures, and low-cut blousy dresses, which are seen as weaponizing their femininity.

While many in the Japanese mainstream continue to view the aggressive traditional male as an ideal persona, fashion magazines, manga, and lifestyle guides support a much wider range of gender expression. *Popeye* magazine's 2011 April issue, for example, highlights floppy hairdos, skirted shorts, A-line silhouettes, and soft color palettes for men that would be the death of the salaryman. The popularity of the herbivore man shows that constructing a new identity often means joining a new tribe that offers safety, companionship, and protection.

LOLITA
BEYOND THE LOOKING GLASS

Literature, like painting, is a powerful tool for identity expression, and the next few images explore how the written word can translate to the real, virtual, and filmic worlds. Japanese cosplay Lolitas dress as hyperfeminine little girls, rejecting the imperfect parts of grown-up life, including the male perception of womanhood. Like twelve-year-old Dolores in Vladimir Nabokov's novel *Lolita*, these cosplayers lean into the assumption that they are young sexual objects seeking the attention of adult men. To the contrary, Japanese teens and women who adorn themselves in bell skirts and doll-like makeup inspired by the Victorian and Rococo eras may be looking for an escape from the male gaze. They hide their adult proportions with platform Mary Janes and silhouettes that obscure their developed breasts and hips. They speak with quiet, "girlish" modesty and embody a passive, childlike attitude through kawaii (cute) design.

There is a precariously sharp edge between a return to childhood and sexual objectification in this cosplay movement. Despite the intensely different reaction from the outside world, Lolitas see their dress as a safe space to express themselves without feeling immense social pressures. Many wear their elaborate decorations and voluminous layers as an escape from their regular day clothes—a reprieve from the stresses of daily life rather than a permanent lifestyle.

Photograph of cosplayer Kelly Ruiz in a cream Lolita ensemble taking afternoon tea in Taipei, Taiwan, in December 2023.

"Lolita, to me, is a form of artistic expression. The clothes are beautiful, fun, and well made.... In my everyday life I am not a 'girly' or 'feminine' person, but I love that I can wear Lolita.... It makes me feel comfortable, since it's not by society's standard, for the male gaze, but my own."[12]

HANNAH DUNCAN
A DOCILE INVENTION

Cosplayers apply their own ideals and desires to their new "skin," deciding which parts of their chosen character are important to them and how they'll interact within their secondary world. But before people invented fictional identities on social media, classical paintings performed the same function. Painters and sitters chose backgrounds, furnishings, and objects of status to elevate the artwork. Artists could correct facial features to match beauty

Portrait of Mrs. John Nicholson (Hannah Duncan) and John Nicholson Jr., painted in 1790 by Charles Wilson Peale, showing an idealized mother in late-eighteenth-century dress.

ideals of the time, and sitters could decide which fashions sent the most advantageous messages. It was social media before social media.

By the eighteenth century, Western women were judged by the ideal of timeless girlhood, and painters faced harsh criticism if their female subjects didn't include visual symbols of virtue, beauty, and obedience that rejected womanhood. Scholar Leslie Reinhardt writes, "Paintings staging the female path to virtue addressed an underlying fear that women had innate, unruly passions—in sexuality, independent behavior, and dress—so threatening to the social order that they must continually be countered and curbed."[15] Beautiful, but not too striking. Educated, but not opinionated. Virtuous, but not prudish. Artists struggled to portray this unrealistic feminine ideal and turned to "invented dress" as a safe solution. These nondescript sitting costumes, as seen in this painting on Hannah, were ill-fitted gowns of ambiguous style and muddy palettes that neutralized female personalities and autonomy. Her son, however, is in a typical eighteenth-century white cotton dress, worn by both male and female children alike.

WE WERE ALL GYRLES ONCE

Contrary to popular belief, babies in the West weren't historically separated by gender until much later in childhood. The term *girlhood* was applied to all children, and boyhood was something half of them grew into. According to one text from 1912, being a girl was the blank slate before adulthood, and "somewhere around the age of ten, the little boy begins to undergo a transformation, which in the girl never takes place at all."[14] In this historical view, boys experience an expansion of the self while girls are timeless children, carrying their innocence, beauty, and obedience into adulthood.

This doesn't mean that little boys dressed like their mothers in gowns and dresses, but that their mothers never stopped dressing like children. From this point of view, it makes sense why, as Jo B. Paoletti, author of two seminal books on dress and gender identity, puts it, "Being a tomboy was an accepted part of childhood for girls, but 'sissy' boys were considered aberrant."[15] By being delicate ruffians, girls showed agency and maturity while gentle boys were interpreted as underdeveloped.

> **"Loosely speaking, the word *girle/gurle/gyrle* was a young child of any gender in Old English and may have come from the word *gyrela/gerela/gierela*, which meant 'garment' and referred to the simple shift toddlers wore after their naked infancy."[16]**

This painting of the Knapp boys from 1833–1834 by Samuel Lovett Waldo and William Jewett shows how young boys were divided according to age through their clothing.

This painting displays all the stages of Victorian childhood for boys in a single family. While each boy transitioned at his own pace, these were generally the stages of boys reaching adulthood:

AGES 0–4 An infant or toddler boy wears dresses with white drawers underneath, indistinguishable from his sisters.

AGES 3–8 The boy is "breeched" and his path into manhood is declared. He starts wearing loose tunic-dresses with trousers that come in a variety of styles, including simple versions of men's frock coats.

AGES 7–13 The boy is "fully breeched" with a short, single-breasted jacket and long trousers.

AGES 14 ONWARD The boy begins to wear more adult fashions, including coats with full skirts or tails. Conversely, girls of this age wear restrictive stays and hoops.

SALLY POTTER
ORLANDO

A historical romp through four centuries of Western manhood and womanhood was the framework for Virginia Woolf's irreverent, four-hundred-year-spanning novel *Orlando*. In the 1993 film based on the book, Tilda Swinton plays the time-traveling, gender-morphing protagonist who changes genders as easily as she (and he) changes time periods. I asked the film's director, Sally Potter, to tell me how she revealed the rich research that created the visual language of the film:

A still from the feature film *Orlando*, with actress Tilda Swinton in a typical sixteenth-century female costume, complete with an all-black corseted bodice, full skirt, and winter cape.

The working principle behind all design decisions in my film *Orlando* was that although the film was set in an accelerated trajectory through four hundred years of British history, it was not a period movie. The story written by Virginia Woolf was, as I saw it, both a meditation on impermanence and an investigation of an immortal being emerging into the present moment. The clothes, designed by Sandy Powell, needed to feel "real" in each period and yet have an intensity that went beyond realism, for this was a story that was "impossible" yet needed to feel believable. (Sandy achieved this balance brilliantly.)

As for Orlando's change of sex in the story, the clothes had to emphasize the formality and elaborate signs of wealth of aristocratic male attire when Orlando was a man, and then the constrictions, exaggerated scale, and display of female clothing when Orlando was a woman.

Virginia Woolf's thesis was that masculinity and femininity are each a kind of learned performance that takes work and practice. Other than the simple biological fact of being born male or female, Virginia Woolf did not give credence to any notion of essential maleness or femaleness, nor did she entertain the idea of any kind of fixed identity. In some sense, she implied, we are all just humans in drag, dancing our way through a labyrinth of time and perpetual change. But along the way we face very different forms of oppression by virtue of how we are defined and perceived.

In the film this manifests as Orlando being bewildered by the expectations society places on him as a man, especially in times of war. He refuses to fight, falls asleep, and wakes up as a woman. But then she is equally baffled and disturbed by the way she is treated, for it seems that as a woman she can only find a future by being attached to a man. The clothes he, and then she, wears in the film needed to echo both a joyful sense of performance and the claustrophobic limits imposed by gender-based oppression. The naked (and now female) Orlando, when stripped of the clothing that defined him as male, can only say "Same person, no difference at all. Just a different sex."[17]

—Sally Potter

A WORLD OF PURE IMAGINATION

Like the character Orlando, able to live within different gendered bodies, video game players can experiment with different identities as they choose their avatars. As digital gaming rose in popularity in the late twentieth century, a brand-new space opened for gender experimentation in a private, anonymous world. Gaming avatars exist between the material and the imaginary, where a player's sense of self is temporary, malleable, and experimental. Virtual avatars allow people to engage in identity tourism in the safety of their communities. They can inhabit characters that have no personal agency but are neutral objects with a set narrative (such as in an animated series) or action list (such as in a game). The immersive element of both is different from reading a novel or watching a movie. "By making the fantasy immersive, the audience is given the illusion of the suspense of the social rules of the society in which they live," say researchers Esther MacCallum-Stewart and Jude Roberts. "An immersive secondary world is one in which literally anything could happen."[18]

One's gender identity (with matching clothing) is something that can be changed at the click of a button, with some games (for example, *Baldur's Gate 3*) featuring multiple gender and body-type choices. The possibilities seem endless. A Roman soldier, iridescent siren, Sailor Moon, Batman, evil necromancer, Wild West cowboy, faerie, alien space pirate…the costume we choose is the person we become. Academic Russell W. Belk notes that "the relative freedom of configuring our avatar bodies has led some to suggest that our avatars represent our ideal selves, possible selves, aspirational selves, or a canvas on which we can 'try out' various alternative selves."[19]

OPPOSITE
Maria Ferreira Kercher's 2024 digital illustration of a gaming avatar, with a wide range of clothing choices encompassing all gender identities, including an ancient Roman gladiator breastplate and a Therian animal mask and paws set.

MINORITY REPORT AND THE FIFTH ELEMENT

Neutral and nonbinary costumes are powerful tools for futuristic visioning in films. The "containment suits" for science fiction action film *Minority Report* are tools of punishment and constraint. Unisex in design, the sleeveless, beige, short bodysuits transform imprisoned "precogs" (mutant humans who can see crimes before they happen) into genderless bodies in the Precrime Hall of Containment. Taking away the individuality of clothing choices, and with them gender identity, is what prison uniforms are designed to do, even when prisoners escape.

In the film *The Fifth Element*, directed by Luc Besson, Milla Jovovich's humanoid fugitive character, Leeloo, runs from the facility where she was made, wearing only bandages.

In the sketches opposite, Leeloo's iconic white bandage costume appears with a 2022 men's Fenty Valentine's Day lingerie set and a 2001 Helmut Lang bright yellow zippered top. All use straps, bandages, and zippers to simultaneously expose and frame the human form and could fit many body types. Because of the construction and materials, these three garments contain no gender identity on the mannequin. But as fashion designer Elizabeth Hawes wrote in her 1942 book *Why Is a Dress?*, "It is impossible to be completely abstract about clothes because they have no life unless they are worn. They must fit onto a body or they do not exist."[20]

This "containment suit" costume from the 2002 feature film *Minority Report* shows how director Steven Spielberg and costume designer Deborah L. Scott visioned genderless uniforms for the future.

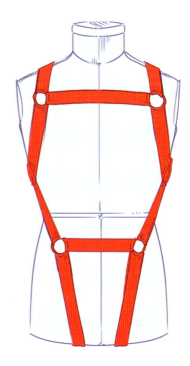

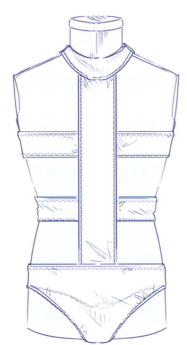

CLOCKWISE FROM TOP LEFT
Fashion designer Helmut Lang's 2001 yellow zippered harness top; Rhianna's Savage X Fenty men's lingerie look for Valentine's Day 2022; Leeloo's escape costume, designed by Jean Paul Gaultier, from the film *The Fifth Element*.

NEUTRALITY

THE ANDROGYNE

W orld-building in video games, fantasy, and science fiction is nothing new; humans have been visioning how gender identity is constructed for millennia. Opposite, the naked form of a two-headed figure with dual genitals, holding an oversized letter *Y*, was one of the subjects of seventeenth-century engraver Michael Maier's *Symbola Aureae Mensae*. The manuscript is 619 pages long, and chapter 6 shows alchemist Albertus Magnus revealing the "Alchemical Androgyne."[21] The letter *Y*, formed from two separate branches converging to become one, symbolized the eternal nature of being, considered to be male and female simultaneously.

Representations of the neutral and intersex body exist in every culture, and examples abound in ancient European times. As long as three thousand years ago, Archaic Greeks painted ceramic pottery depicting intersex individuals, Dionysus was a mischievous genderfluid Greek God, and the Romans sculpted marble forms with both male and female attributes. A contro-versial original text by ancient Roman writer Cassius Dio details how second-century CE Roman emperor Elagabalus, still a teenager, hoped for surgery that would affirm his identity as a woman.[22]

Many versions of the androgyne origin story exist. In *The Symposium*, Plato's 385–370 BCE semi-comic play that imagines an evening of conversation between fellow philosophers about philia (love), eros (desire), and same-sex love between an erastes (adult male lover) and eromenos

(the adolescent beloved), Aristophanes
shares the mythology of the androgynoi
(androgynes) and their origin story.[23]

> The sexes were not two as they are
> now, but originally three in number;
> there was man, woman, and the union
> of the two, having a name correspond-
> ing to this double nature, which had
> once a real existence, but is now lost…
> the man was originally the child of the
> sun, the woman of the earth and the
> man-woman of the moon, which is
> made up of the sun and earth.[24]

In this retelling, an angry Zeus cleaved
the male and female being in half, and the
androgyne disappeared from Earth, but

not from human imagination, resurfacing
over and over in art, literature, and popular
culture. For instance, a small 1550s oil painting in a private collection depicts this phenomenon of male and female halves attached
at the back, facing opposite directions (naked
except for the male figure wearing shoes with
spurs and a red hat!). Opposite is another
example of this early world-building: a dual
figure from an Italian fifteenth-century
manuscript, wearing a "mi-parti" (color-
blocked) knee-length "cote," or outer layer,
divided into quarters of red, gold, black,
and bronze colors, highlighting how artists
have strived to make the intangible visible
for millennia.

רָאְלַמ
THE MESSENGERS

A single eye carried aloft on wings; blue, cherub-faced clouds; intangible water vapor; an oval of golden light—these are some of the ways that Byzantine, medieval, and Renaissance painters chose to depict angels. In biblical terms, angels are heavenly, neutral beings unless they are called to come to Earth. When they do, how should they look and what clothes should they wear? In *The Annunciation*, Renaissance painter Jan van Eyck depicted an androgynous young man framed in rainbow-hued, feathered wings and wearing ornate, ornamented, red robes—a fashion atypical of the mid-1400s. The angel's curly, long, blond hair is crowned with gold and jewels. Part ecclesiastical, part fantastical, van Eyck's Archangel Gabriel is otherworldly and superhuman.

Representations of angels tended toward male human forms, but the Virgin Mary was often surrounded by a court of winged female angels. The Hebrew of the Old Testament had gendered binary pronouns, and the typical pronoun used for angels was masculine. The archaic Hebrew word for angel is *malach* (רָאְלַמ), meaning "messenger." In ancient Greek, the word was *angelos*, also meaning messenger, and in Latin, *angelus*. Modern theorists claim angels as gender neutral, but the clothes and original pronouns tell a different story: neutral in heaven, mostly masculine on Earth.

OPPOSITE
Jan van Eyck's painting *The Annunciation*, from 1434–1436, shows Archangel Gabriel, a neutral being, in earthly form as an androgynous messenger from heaven.

스님
BUDDHIST MONASTICS

The icy blue of a predawn sky has yet to brush the heavens by the time most Korean Buddhist monastics, or seunim, rise at four in the morning to the sound of a handheld wooden temple drum. They don their robe-like gray-and-brown linen garment—the hanbok—and sensible shoes, then gather for morning meditation. Regardless of the monastic's gender or sex, their goal is the same: total neutrality through detachment from the self and, therefore, from suffering. Monastics of all genders shear their heads, and in many sects of Buddhism, from Korea to Japan to Tibet, routines and robes are nearly identical for men and women. Becoming selfless means letting go of gender identity, which is tied to earthly attachments. Casting off gendered garments is the next step. As Minjee Kim, co-editor of *Dress History of Korea*, notes, the

soul is thought to be genderless. She makes the connection that some Korean garments were considered unisex until recently, like the Korean coat.[25]

Ninety-two-year-old Tibetan monastic Mingyur Lama from the Dechen Ling nunnery in Qinghai continues a millennia-old Theravada tradition of wearing chos gö (religious clothing) shared by all genders. The garment is dyed in bold colors— a beautiful by-product of using abundant local, natural dyestuffs to create red, maroon, yellow, and orange hues. She also puts on a dhonka, a maroon, cold-weather, upper robe with cap sleeves piped in blue. Many of the garments she wears for ceremonial or day-to-day life, such as her maroon shemdap skirt, are inspired by the "pure cloth" the Buddha asked his first followers to make from patchwork scraps. Adherents no longer scavenge in cremation piles for their fabrics, but modern Buddhist patchwork cloth remains a symbol of spiritual neutrality and detachment from the world.

OPPOSITE TOP
A group of monks wear genderless gray "hanbok" robes and wide-brimmed hats while walking to Seokguram Grotto, South Korea.

OPPOSITE BOTTOM
Ninety-two-year-old Mingyur Lama, photographed in 2018, wears gender-neutral "chos gö" religious dress in saffron and crimson hues.

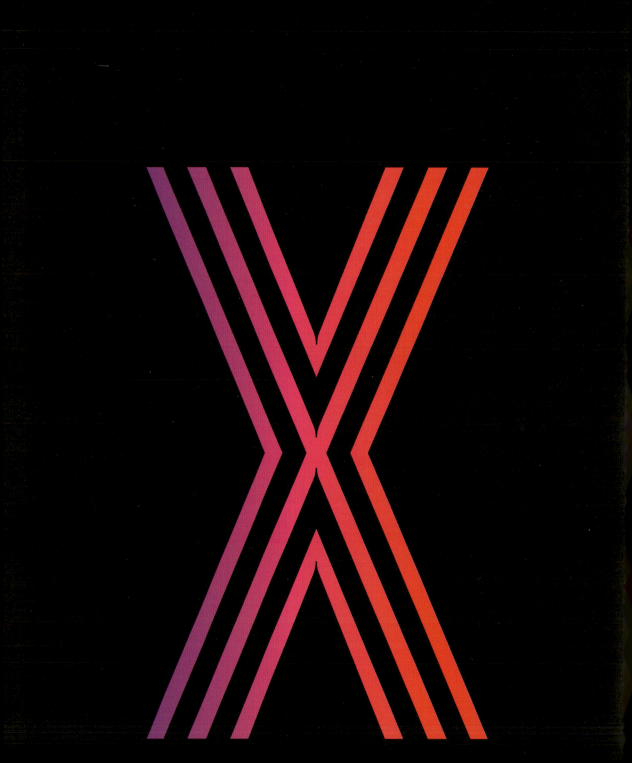

(UNISEX)

PATONS Promise

6302
1/- (5p)

Dress: 33-40 in. (84-101 cm)
Sweater: 37-44 in. (94-111 cm)

*U*nisex (defined as "one," from the Latin *uni* or *unus*) means different things to different cultures. We all know the word *unisex*, but what does it really mean to us? Unisex fashion occupies an extremely specific place in Western culture, a place that is reliant on the binary. Dress historian Minjee Kim uses the word *unisex* rather than *neutral* to describe a Korean coat worn by both binary genders, and notes that this garment was considered unisex until recently.[1] Unisex in science-fictional visioning can refer to genderless uniforms and costumes, and unisex children's dress supports the modern global cultural trend of allowing gender identity to manifest in more genderfluid ways (think boys in princess dresses in the preschool sandbox or girls in overalls hanging from an elementary school play structure). So what is the difference between unisex and neutral, and how do the differences influence fashion?

A conversation with writer and dress historian Jo B. Paoletti, who has researched how sex and gender identity affect dress, reveals her thoughts on "the tremendous power of the gender-shaping abilities of clothing."[2] In her 2015 book *Sex and Unisex*, Paoletti writes that unisex clothing really emphasizes the binary between male and female bodies, rather than neutralizing it.[3] Western unisex fashions trended in the postwar counterculture 1960s and '70s, allowing space for new ways of self-presentation. In this context, unisex dress is important as a way of thinking that helps define or blur boundaries. As Paoletti observes, "If sexuality can be on the spectrum, then clothes can do something else besides differentiate the gender binary."[4] Binaries may seem simple but are not, and a dive into unisex clothes reveals this and asks the question: What happens when typical erogenous zones change? Or can they?

Paoletti took up the invitation to revisit the idea of unisex for this book, and shares how it is just one of many labels used to signify when something is not based on the binary male–female, masculine– feminine construction. "The interesting (and frustrating) thing about all of these concepts is that they rely on the binary. After all, how can something be resisted or rejected unless it exists in the first place?"[5] When Paoletti began her research fifty years ago, she encouraged readers to not ignore the binary but consider the possibility of accepting the basis for it, with all of its flaws and caveats.

Yes, humans are superficially classifiable as male or female. "Superficially" because sex is determined by how we look on the outside. But some of us are not immediately identifiable as one or the other. One baby in five thousand is born with ambiguous genitals, meaning they are not clearly male or female. If we look beneath the surface, there are hidden aspects of sex (hormones, for example) that also complicate the "truth" of the binary. Adam and Eve notwithstanding, belief in two distinct sexes ignores these facts.[6]

Paoletti offers further thoughts on how the trends of unisex fashion might not last the test of time but can encourage discussion about gender expressions:

If biological sex is not a duality, how can we justify binarizing (for lack of a better word) sexuality, gender roles, or gender identity? Yet we do. If most humans have bodies that fit one stereotype or another, how can we not? Unisex clothing—even just as it existed between 1965 and 1975—tells us just how complex gender expression can be.[7]

One straightforward example of the unisex phenomenon is the "temple garments" (modesty undergarments) worn by members of the Church of Jesus Christ of Latter-day Saints. In the early 1970s, as women's liberation in America was daily news, slacks for women were allowed by church leadership but unisex dress was discouraged. Writer Katie Clark Blakesley notes that church officials encouraged men and women to wear modest fashions that made male and female distinctions very clear, unlike the androgynous counterculture looks that were sweeping the nation.[8] The binary pink-and-blue packaging illustrated opposite advertises a set of undergarments that, functionally, can fit all genders, like the biblical "kitoneth" (similar to the "chiton" mentioned above). Rory Scanlon, a costume designer, historian, and member of the Church of Jesus Christ of Latter-day Saints, spoke with me about these infamous underlayers.[9] In the early 1900s, temple garments—knitted wear covering the entire body, with buttons at the torso and a drop-down flap at the backside—were originally unisex "union suits" worn for modesty. Nowadays, they are a pair of undershorts with a simple short-sleeved top. They are functionally unisex but not culturally unisex. My conversations with LDS dress historians in Salt Lake City, Utah, revealed that they would never swap their garments with their wife or husband, no matter how similar they were.[10] "Why is this so confusing?" Paoletti exclaims. "Because it's complicated!"[11]

All of the images in this chapter are complicated and sometimes confusing in how they represent the unisex—that's why it's so tricky to define, and it's why Paoletti has devoted years of research to the topic. This short chapter starts with a cheeky 1920s postcard of a fashionable "boyish" gal and her "girlish" boyfriend who twin in their matching fashions, but it's really their androgynous body types, hairstyles, and poses that unify them. Influential 1960s and '70s fashion designer Rudi Gernreich popularized the concept of unisex with plain old sex, marketing, and erogenous zones. The *sex* in *unisex* was his actual goal. Finally, case studies of aprons, jumpsuits, turtlenecks, loincloths, tunics, and sandals show us how hidden gender roles are found in clothes that seem unisex on the surface.

Digital illustration of the Church of Jesus Christ of Latter-day Saints temple garment packaging, 2024.

ALMOST UNISEX

America and Europe flirted with unisex fashion throughout the 1920s, a time of reexamining gender roles after the turmoil of WWI. This trend was mirrored in caricatures and cartoons of women mistaken for men and vice versa, as seen on this 1924 postcard featuring a cigarette-smoking modern girlfriend and boyfriend in matching outfits. Post–WWI young women (accustomed to the freedom of working at factories, driving, smoking cigarettes, and playing sports while men were at war) cropped their hair, wore knee-length skirts and menswear-inspired trousers for the first time in American history, and rejected corsets and hourglass waistlines.

Bust minimizers popped up in department stores as women searched for a clean, sleek, boyish silhouette. Androgynous male actors graced the newly emerging silver screen—a drastic change from the hypermasculine archetype that WWI posters promoted. The boyfriend in the postcard has the idealized androgynous body type for 1920s unisex fashion: athletic and lithe. The height difference between the couple also tells a story; in the postcard, the girlfriend is taller than the boyfriend, which was atypical for the binary stereotype at the time.

But transitions in men's and women's clothing meant that a true unisex look was not achieved. Many fashionable young men wore long, ultrawide trousers (up to 23 inches around one hem) called Oxford bags, while many women wore knee-grazing dresses and skirts. This meant that the fashion of the previous decades of men in straight-leg trousers and women in floor-length, full skirts was gleefully reversed.

OPPOSITE
1924 Inter-Art Co. postcard of a couple wearing matching Fair Isle sweaters with similar cropped hairstyles. The girlfriend wears an ultra-modern knee-length skirt; the boyfriend is in fashionable wide-legged trousers.

"Me and my Boy Friend, My Boy Friend and me,
There isn't much difference between us, but he
Wears his Hair and his Skirts a bit longer than me."

RUDI GERNREICH
SEX SELLS

Fashion designer Rudi Gernreich, born in Austria during the 1920s flapper era, revisited androgynous and gender-bending dress in 1960s Los Angeles. He created some of the most controversial garments in an era that was already androgynous compared to the highly binary dress of 1950s America. But Gernreich took his designs to the extreme with gendered garments like the pubikini, a sheer panty that revealed dyed pubic hair; the monokini, a topless bathing suit meant to free women from the gender binary; and a one-piece thong swimsuit for men. Unisex jumpsuits and whimsical matching lounge sets for men and women came with coordinated face-obscuring headpieces.[12]

Revealing erogenous zones and concealing faces were two ways Gernreich tried to liberate the body. In this photo shoot for the 1970s Unisex Series, an androgynous effect is achieved with faces covered by turtlenecks

Rudi Gernreich Unisex Series, 1970, photographed by Patricia Faure.

and heads shaved bald. The appearance of both the male and female models is almost unisex, except for the feminine curve of the woman's breast.

THE TUTA

The TuTa—designed for all people, utilitarian and utopian, and easy to make from inexpensive fabric—was advertised as the perfect unisex garment. Futurist artist Thayaht (born Ernesto Michahelles) designed the jumpsuit with his brother RAM (born Ruggero Alfredo Michahelles) in 1919. The word *tutta* in Italian translates to *one*, *whole*, or *unified*, and the TuTa is almost universal. Since he lived through WWI, Thayaht would have understood the unifying camaraderie of military uniforms like flight suits and jumpsuits worn by soldiers and airmen, and postwar utopian dreams of a new world order.

Thayaht wrote that "the TuTa is designed as a universal garment for 'EVERYONE,' 'FOR ALL PEOPLE,' from which then a 'T' decays, for 'TUTI,' 'FOR ALL PEOPLE'; the lost consonant 'T' regenerates and is reabsorbed and found in the model itself, which has the shape of a 'T.'"[15] The Thayaht & RAM Archive in Florence, Italy, now curated by Riccardo Michahelles, holds a rich history of the TuTa.

"Thayaht in TuTa," 1920. Thayaht models his own TuTa.

Thayaht's ideal was the same jumpsuit for all people, except he designed a women's version of the TuTa with a skirt (the original was only for men and boys, as noted on its pattern). Thayaht also designed a two-piece set, the BiTuTa, and all variations could be paired with his sandali di Firenze, or Florentine sandals.

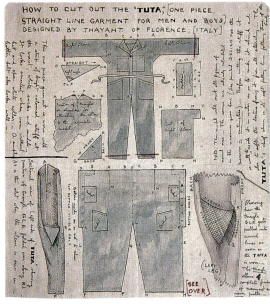

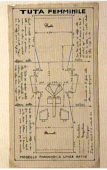 

ABOVE
"The Female TuTa," 1920. The pattern for a women's TuTa shows how the smock-like dress with practical pockets can be cut from one continuous piece of cloth.

TOP
"RAM Tuttintuta," 1920. Thayaht's postcard illustration shows a group of Italian citizens stepping into a hopeful, futuristic world.

ABOVE
"How to Cut the TuTa." This free pattern was printed in a Florentine newspaper in 1920, requiring only one rectangle of fabric measuring 4.5 by 0.7 meters, seven buttons, and a belt.

THE NDEBELE APRON
BLANK SLATE

An ancient example of garments that could be worn by all genders, aprons seem utterly unisex. But some time spent in the archives with the curators of the Seattle Art Museum's marvelous collection of embellished leather and cloth aprons reveals a different story.[14] Turkana aprons aren't gendered because they are a garment specific to women; Turkana men can wear a form of apron too. They are gendered because the way they are decorated and encoded means they are the visual symbol of the unique path of a woman's journey from childhood to adulthood.

In Kenya and South Africa, traditional waist aprons from the Turkana and Ndebele tribes are like billboards: they advertise biological gender, age, marital status, wealth, and even the opinions of the wearer (some aprons carry protest and political messages). In Ndebele aprons, a wide variety of materials like leather, glass beads, ostrich eggs, iron, raffia, animal horn, and colored plastic are used for self-expression and creativity.

Ndebele aprons document the three steps of a girl's journey to womanhood. A prepubescent girl wears a triangular

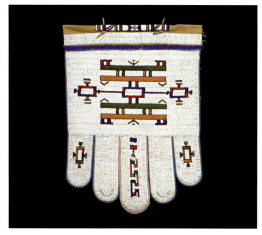

The striking glass beadwork on the mid-twentieth-century leather and cloth Ndebele apron, the "Ijogolo," is traditionally worn by married women.

leather apron made of leather with a hand-beaded waist strap of ostrich egg beads. (Young boys wear a similar triangular apron, highlighting how childhood dress is often less gendered than adult dress.) Upon reaching puberty, a girl switches to a square apron with intricate adornment. When married, a Ndebele woman receives a blank apron from her husband's family and adds the beading and "flaps" or "fingers" that communicate her status as a wife.

NDEBELE APRON LANGUAGE

GHABI — a simple, prepubescent, one-piece, triangular apron
PEPITU — an adolescent apron, square, with adornment but no flaps
IJOGOLO — a married women's apron, elaborately embellished, with up to five flaps
MAPOTO — a ceremonial apron

TEES, FLIP-FLOPS, AND UNDIES

These three ancient garments—a T-shaped tunic, a loincloth, and a pair of woven sandals—look neutral at first glance. Couldn't a person of any gender identity wear them in the same way, with the same practical functions? They seem like the Tibetan monastic's garments in their neutrality. But the moment they are worn, social and cultural rules gender these garments.

Linen Smock

Pictograms of T-shaped garments have been found in ancient Egyptian writing, looking just like a sketch of a T-shirt. The twenty-first century is arguably the century of the T-shirt, and most would say the garment is unisex. Almost everyone has a stack in their closet. The cut of women's and men's tees are very similar, and fashion designers delving into unisex or gender-neutral garments rely on the T-shirt shape—full-length or cropped, long-sleeved or short—as an essential basic. This ancient Egyptian tunic (kalasiris) made from extremely fine pleated linen is the ancestor of modern tees worn on the streets of cities like Mumbai, Bangkok, and Cape Town. Dated to 2323–2150 BCE, this kalasiris could have been worn by men or women. But the wearer's choice of headdresses, jewelry,

mantles (robe-like overlayers), footwear, and hairstyles automatically would have identified them as male or female.

Sandals

These woven papyrus reed sandals from a Theban tomb near modern-day Luxor, Egypt, are so well preserved it's hard to believe they were handmade in 1580–1479 BCE. A very early precursor to modern flip-flops (like the famous Havaianas from Brazil), the shape and material remained the same for men, women, and children, but the decorations were gendered.

Loincloth

The most unisex of all the garments was worn only by men. The shendyt (loincloth) was a simple triangular waist wrapping, varying in length from a lower-class groin covering to upper-class ceremonial versions that fell to the knee and were accessorized by a decorative belt. This small, folded loincloth dates to 1425–1353 BCE and features fine, rolled-edge hand stitching, which developed in ancient Egypt only after 3000 BCE. It would have been worn by a worker or middle-class individual, but only a man. Respectable women wore the kalasiris, and for them, a shendyt would have been considered cross-dressing.

TOP
Linen kalasiris, Museum of Fine Arts, Boston.

BELOW
Reed sandals, Metropolitan Museum of Art, New York.

BOTTOM
Linen loincloth, Museum Egizio, Turin, Italy.

1899 CE
INDUSTRIAL REVOLUTION

As the West raced toward industrialization during the nineteenth century, men left the home in record numbers to work in offices, factories, and abroad. Women were not only considered property of a man's household, but they were expected to run it as well! In 1899, economist Thorstein Veblen noted how a woman's feminine dress directly reflected the morality and status of a respectable middle-class family, while men were expected to dress modestly in dark colors accented with crisp, clean linen. Fashion was seen as frivolous and color was seen as decorative, so both became women's domains.

1910 CE
GIBSON GIRLS

Rejecting the linen smocks of Pre-Raphaelite dress were the aggressively feminine Gibson Girls of the late nineteenth century (named after the famed Charles Dana Gibson's illustrations of hyperfeminine women). The two styles were polar opposites. Gibson Girls prized tightly corseted, narrow waists that were emphasized by pigeon-breasted bustlines, which enhanced the new fashion of fine cotton shirtwaist blouses. All this was topped off with a bird's nest of hair and finished with delicate, pointed satin boots. It's no wonder that the images of Gibson Girls were used to market everything from soap to socks.

UNISEX TO BINARY

1848 CE
AESTHETIC DRESS

Artists, painters, and literary figures rebelled against the respectable, gender-rigid industrialization of Europe's cities. In 1848 a group of artists, yearning for the simpler design style of the Middle Ages, established the Pre-Raphaelite Brotherhood. They rejected tight corsetry in women's clothing in favor of natural fibers and healthier garment shapes, and Aesthetic fashion became one of the most recognizable elements of the Pre-Raphaelite movement. Photographed by Julia Margaret Cameron from 1840 to 1860, Pre-Raphaelite women wore unstructured linen dresses and left their hair loose. Painter Alphonse Mucha reverted to wearing traditional Czech peasant shirts, and playwright Oscar Wilde, wearing eighteenth-century breeches and green velvet jackets, toured the United States in 1882, lecturing on aestheticism and inspiring a wave of similarly dressed American aesthetes in his wake.

1947 CE
DIOR'S HOURGLASS

Fashion is often a pendulum, not a straight line. When WWII ended in 1945, fashion trends encouraged women back to waist cinchers, petticoats, and heels—and out of trousers. Men left behind their military uniforms for wide-shouldered suits with nipped waists. Male dress reinforced virility and capability, while women's dress prioritized beauty, morality, and femininity, influenced by Christian Dior's hourglass-shaped New Look collection in 1947. Gender binaries were pushed to the limit: men in suits at work, women in aprons at home.

2022 CE
RISE OF THE TRADWIFE

The "tradwife" movement hearkened back to an idealized prefeminist era. Primarily white, Western tradwives posted videos of home cooking, vegetable raising, and child-rearing, while their husbands were the family's single earners. As tradwives hand-churned butter while wearing newborns in slings, they donned New Look silhouettes that referenced 1950s hyperfemininity or gingham prairie dresses of a mythical American past. The irony lies in how many tradwives leveraged millions of followers into successful, lucrative, influencer careers.

1914–1918 AND 1939–1945 CE
THE WORLD WARS

During WWI (1914–1918) and WWII (1939–1945), the sartorial symbols of patriotism were coveralls, dungarees, and jumpsuits. Regardless of gender, citizens pitched in with the war effort, and their clothes were designed for the war effort, not fashion. During WWI, Land Girls took over agricultural jobs in men's absence and were largely drawn from the working classes. Fashion was put by the wayside, but paradoxically it was expected that women keep up appearances to keep up morale. Rosie the Riveter, in her coveralls and headscarf, became the face of WWII's working women. In both wars, military khaki and uniforms were worn on the streets while munitions clothes (coverall dresses or jumpsuits) were acceptable for dinner out.

2020 CE
THE PANDEMIC

Bonding over isolation and social distancing in 2020, Americans camouflaged themselves in disposable masks, fleece onesies, slippers, and Crocs. Gender signifiers were minimal as the population shifted into crisis mode. Unisex loungewear, globally amplified by social media, became a symbol of solidarity. Leaving behind blankets and slippers in post-pandemic 2022 meant reentering society and work, like soldiers leaving behind their uniforms or Land Girls their coveralls. A new relationship with clothes emerged, and social media rapidly fragmented these changes into a blizzard of globally accessible micro trends.

(BINARY)

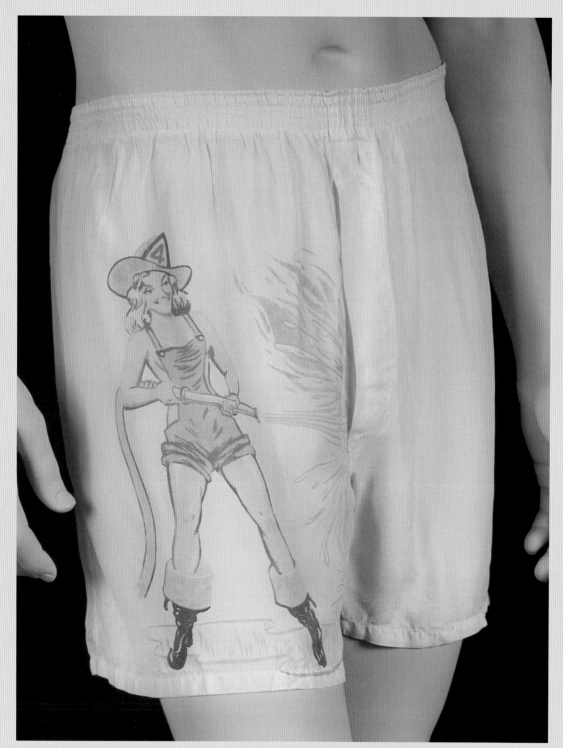

Hand-painted woven rayon boxer
shorts manufactured by Manning
around 1950–1959, in the collection
of the Fashion Institute of Design
and Merchandising Museum.

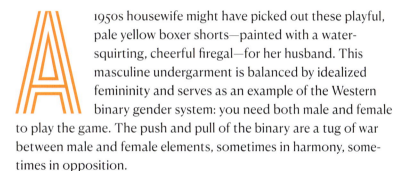

A 1950s housewife might have picked out these playful, pale yellow boxer shorts—painted with a water-squirting, cheerful firegal—for her husband. This masculine undergarment is balanced by idealized femininity and serves as an example of the Western binary gender system: you need both male and female to play the game. The push and pull of the binary are a tug of war between male and female elements, sometimes in harmony, sometimes in opposition.

From the Latin *bini* or *two together*, the binary by its very definition involves two parts. But even if the language is clear, history hasn't always been consistent. Fashions change and flip, so a color or style associated with a masculine trait at one point in time might change to a feminine one a century later. A 1918 *Ladies' Home Journal* article declared,

> There has been a great diversity of debate on the subject, but the generally accepted rule is pink for the boys, and blue for the girls. The reason is that pink, being a more decided and stronger color, is more suitable for the boy, while blue, which is more delicate and dainty, is prettier for the girl.[1]

When the binary doesn't work for someone, or when there is no outlet for authentic self-expression, binary fashion restricts us. There is nothing wrong with binary dressing except when it offers no options for individuals who don't align with one gender role.

Rites of passage, generational change, ceremonies, and celebrations show how the binary is deeply encoded in Western society. They play a big part in cementing the binary in culture. The American post–WWII high school, where this chapter begins, amplifies the rituals that reinforce postpubescent binary roles. Beauty pageants and weddings drive the binary home but can be subverted to suit new ways of creating gender-expansive spaces. Later in the chapter, photographs show how in the 1960s and '70s, American and British counterculture movements disrupted the gender binary, and fashion historian Chloe Chapin explores gendered menswear. The neoclassical binary and Japanese twentieth-century dress show how the binary is encoded, and finally, a short history of men in skirts leads to a short history of the kilt. The chapter begins with Troy Morgan, an artist working in the digital space, and his visioning of the binary rituals of American adolescence.

TROY MORGAN'S HOMECOMING HORROR

Ask any American about high school, and the memories will start flowing. The number of movies, books, TV series, and comics depicting the highs and lows of American high school is evidence enough that the rituals and ceremonies that happen during those years are deeply embedded in our cultural consciousness. High school mirrors rites of passage, from starting high school (leaving childhood for puberty) and going to prom (a faux wedding) to attending homecoming football events (war games and soldiers returning from battle) to becoming cheerleaders (women waiting on the home front) to graduating (leaving puberty to become an adult).

These three paintings (including the one on pages 76 and 77) from visual artist Troy Morgan mix ancient symbolism with modern American imagery to comment on the rituals of Western life. I spoke with Morgan about his process for the series:

> Drawing from the small-town culture and institutions of my youth, as well as the imagery of the satanic-panic era, I created surreal landscapes that weave together religious ceremonies, high school celebrations, and fairy tales, blurring the lines between occultism, homecoming parades, witchcraft, and prom nights. The paintings and animations are both inspired by the iconographic imagery of my Catholic upbringing, as well as the horror films and transgressive cinema of the 1970s and '80s that provided a counter-narrative and critique of these traditions. Characters are cloaked in their familiar, hierarchical uniforms, but take on an aura of spiritualism reminiscent of the symbolist paintings of the late nineteenth century. A homecoming that could belong in a Hammer Film horror movie.[2]

BENDING THE RULES: FASHION BEYOND THE BINARY

GREASE
GOOD GIRL GONE BAD

If there is one movie that simultaneously defines and parodies the binary rituals of American high school, it's *Grease*. Shot in 1978 in Los Angeles, *Grease* crystallizes four years of 1950s high school binary fashion into one peppy, heartfelt, iconic musical starring Olivia Newton-John as Sandy Olsson and John Travolta as Danny Zuko. Throughout the movie, Danny wears variations on the classic 1950s rocker look—blue jeans, tees, leather jackets—and adds a dark prom tux with hot pink dress shirt and cream letterman's sweater for key plot points as he tries to dress to impress Sandy. Meanwhile, Sandy's costumes go from innocent Australian newcomer to streetwise high school grad in the space of 105 minutes. A comparison of two drive-in movie scene stills from the film reveals her character's trajectory.

Albert Wolsky, the film's costume designer, is ninety-five now but shared his experiences with me during a February 2025 phone chat as if he had just wrapped filming, rather than forty-seven years ago.

For Wolsky, the tightrope-like balance between respectable and provocative was at the heart of his design, especially since dance and body movement anchor the action of the film. While John Travolta's seductive moves were a consistent force in the film, Wolsky remembers that Olivia Newton-John could not wait to shed her prim and proper looks (like her demure white prom dress with modest sheer capelet) for her final carnival costume, where her red high-heel mules and all-black biker chic meant she could channel the rebelliousness of Rizzo. The binary push and pull of Danny and Sandy's costumes depends on Wolsky's brilliant design work to broadcast Western ideals of morality. Conforming to the gender binary in the beginning of the film meant that Sandy had something to rebel against in the end.

OPPOSITE TOP
For the first drive-in movie scene, Sandy's look is prim little girl: ponytail with hair ribbon, pastel top with Peter Pan collar, green calf-length skirt, bobby socks, and two-toned saddle shoes.

OPPOSITE BOTTOM
Sandy's second drive-in movie look is a polar opposite of the first. Instead of pastels, she's in all black, twinning with her man in motorcycle jackets. Instead of a girlish ponytail, Sandy's hair is wild, sexy, and rocker cool. A red lip signals womanhood rather than girlhood.

CARRIE
TEENAGE RAGE

Released two years earlier than *Grease* and taking high-school rejection many steps further, is *Carrie*, the 1976 horror movie starring Sissy Spacek. Young outcast Carrie White has no hopes of going to the prom until Tommy Ross, the boyfriend of a popular girl, asks her to go as a mean-spirited prank. Costume designer Rosanna Norton chose the palest pink slip dress for Carrie's transformational prom look so that the gallons of pig blood dumped on Carrie as she is crowned prom queen had maximum impact. Tommy and Carrie, like Danny and Sandra, conform to the modern wedding binary of formal tuxedo for men and a pale-colored, long, feminine dress for women.

In both *Grease* and *Carrie*, the characters have no choice beside binary roles and binary clothing. Through this lens we see two very different coping skills: while Sandra transforms herself from good girl to rebel through her fashion and survives within the binary system, Carrie burns herself and everyone else to the ground. Nowadays, the gender binary is blurring quickly in America, and the LGBTQ+ community is reclaiming these ceremonial and celebratory events with alt proms, menswear-inspired prom fashion for tomboys, and genderfluid prom looks combining, for example, a buttoned-up shirt and tie with a sparkly ball gown skirt.

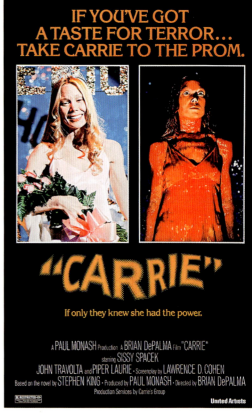

Carrie movie poster from 1976. Directed by Brian De Palma and starring Sissy Spacek, Piper Laurie, and Amy Irving, the film explores how female rage and coming of age collide as a group of teens navigate the popularity contest ritual of American prom.

LILLI WOLFF
THE MAIFEST

Like stereotypical Western childhood rituals—where young girls attend family weddings in voluminous party dresses, hair ribbons, and ladylike shoes and young boys are scrubbed clean before they put on a little suit, shirt, and tie—beauty pageants, balls, and proms rely on the binary for structure. For the teenage "young lady," debutante and festival dresses were a rite of passage. Dressmaker Lilli Wolff designed this floaty yellow 1950s confection of a gown worn on a white-and-gold parade float gliding down a sunny street in Berman, Texas. The ladies sit in pastel dresses, while the young men wear white tuxedo jackets, black bow ties, and black satin and striped dress trousers. It's a procession, a ritual mimicking a royal coronation, to present new youth to society.

Designer Lilli Wolff's Maifest debutante dress sketch with detailed notes and questions for the client, 1950/1969.

A chance meeting with Annette Becker, director of the Texas Fashion Collection, at a dress history conference revealed more about the archives of Lilli Wolff, a dress designer who escaped Nazi persecution as a Jew and lesbian by immigrating to the United States during WWII. Becker described the path that Wolff took to Dallas, Texas, from "her career as a theater costume designer in Vienna and her escape to New York City, where she made pageant gowns for Miss America contestants and winners, to her relocation to Dallas, where she was a custom dressmaker."[3] Perhaps Wolff's success was partly because of her identity as an immigrant and LGBTQ+ individual—it gave her an outsider's understanding of these unique American rituals.

Maifest celebration float, Texas, 1958, carrying debutantes and their escorts.

BRENHAM WHOSLE GRO CO INC

Like proms, beauty pageants and debutante balls are changing. Since 2012 Miss Universe has welcomed transgender contestants, and since 2022 the organization has had its first female owner, Jakkaphong Jakrajutatip.

OPPOSITE
A delicate, 1958 Maifest debutante dress, crafted from yellow organza with peau de soie, with light and dark green velvet ribbon and multicolored faux flowers and leaves, crafted by dressmaker Mati Driessen.

ABOVE
Maifest celebration float, Texas, 1958, carrying debutantes and their escorts.

WHITE WEDDING

Camelot is how Jackie Kennedy described the John F. Kennedy presidency to *Life* magazine in 1963, after her husband was shot.[4] The word *Camelot* conjures up medieval castles, Lady Guinevere, the Knights of King Arthur, and, more importantly for this wedding photograph, the romantic notion of a valiant, capable (male) warrior protecting a virtuous, helpless (female) maiden. Within the traditional binary, a wedding is the ultimate ritual, and the wedding of two socially powerful families, the Bouviers and the Kennedys, was as royal as American democracy could get.

Rites of passage like attending proms, competing in beauty pageants, and playing sports (as well as culture's expectations for childhood for boys and girls) all lead up to this moment where men and women perform their ultimate binary roles.

African American fashion designer Ann Lowe created Jackie's 1953 wedding dress from ivory silk taffeta with fifty yards of circular flounces.[5] Everyone, from the groom to Jackie's mother, Janet Auchincloss, had opinions about (and expectations for) Jackie's dress, which combined the visual language of prom, a society debut, and an almost-royal wedding into one symbolic gown. John, a senator at the time, wore morning dress: a cutaway coat with a boutonniere and white handkerchief, hickory-striped trousers, a gray waistcoat, and, notably, a pair of blue Brooks Brothers boxer shorts. As many traditional 1950s postwar families did, the couple went on to set up a home, have children, and fulfill their cultural binary roles as American "royalty."

John F. Kennedy and Jacqueline Bouvier Kennedy conform to binary roles and fashions in this 1953 wedding portrait, with a narrow, dark silhouette for the groom and an hourglass-shaped bodice with a full, floor-length skirt for the bride.

SUBURBAN BLISS

A white picket fence lines the green clover lawn of a home painted buttercream yellow with white eyelet shutters. Two children ride cherry red bicycles on the sidewalk while their spotted Jack Russell terrier barks and wags his tail. Their father waves as he mows the lawn, and their mother smiles through the window as she does dishes. This is the picturesque, *Mad Men*–like tableau of suburban life after WWII. War-weary Americans ached for order and predictability in the 1950s and escaped into the domestic bliss promoted by postwar advertising. Hypermasculine and hyperfeminine gender roles gave both citizens and the US government a sense of stability while the future remained precarious. Many men returned from WWII physically and mentally damaged while the women at home had become independent and well trained in the workforce.

As society tried to reset the binary, men's and women's roles diverged to the extreme in America. Chores were divided by whether they occurred inside or outside of the home. A husband might take out the trash, mow the lawn, and grill on the barbecue, while his wife might vacuum, fold the laundry, and cook dinner. In fashion, men's shoulders widened and their hips narrowed, while women's skirts inflated and their waists shrank. Colors were again divided by gender, with blue assigned to boys and pink to girls. The resulting division of the sexes became a defining element of the American Dream.

BENDING THE RULES: FASHION BEYOND THE BINARY

"Suburban Bliss," digital illustrations by
50s Vintage Dame, July 2024.

THE RAINBOW FAMILY
SHARED CLOSETS

A pair of jeans in the late 1960s might have started their life hugging the waist of a good old American farmer tending dusty fields and mucking stalls. A few years later, once they were too worn down and had done their job, perhaps they'd make their way to a flea market. A young man might buy them, though they're covered in holes and fraying. He'd cut the side seams open to widen the legs below the knees and perform surgery to transform those old straight-leg jeans into a garment with a message. In the years to come, the bell-bottoms might have found their way through thrift stores and hand-me-downs to the Rainbow Family, a counterculture activist group, seen in this 1976 snapshot. Clothiers in the 1960s considered bell-bottoms too risky to manufacture for men, so rebels cobbled them together from naval uniforms and work jeans.

The bell-bottom shape was widespread by the early 1970s and became integrated into business suits and leisure-wear, and has dipped in and out of fashion, most recently on rapper Kendrick Lamar, who wore a pair of blue denim Celine bell-bottoms while performing in New Orleans, Louisiana, at Super Bowl LIX in 2025.

Together with long hair, bell-bottoms played a pivotal role in creating a gender-neutral look for the baby boom generation, paving the way for men and women to share wardrobe basics such as T-shirts, jeans, and sandals. Couples from the 1950s who had strictly divided closets and domestic roles found that their children wanted to share closets instead. People across genders experienced a bombastic explosion of self-expression and individuality thanks to the convergence of closets. The rules of fashion weren't as restrictive as they had been in previous decades, so rather than conform-ing to a binary uniform, they challenged the status quo, claiming that all fashion, all art, and all beauty were for all people.

The Rainbow Family gathers at the Chief Mountain International Border Crossing between Alberta and Montana for a peaceful celebration on July 4, 1976.

BENDING THE RULES: FASHION BEYOND THE BINARY

A POSTMODERN COUPLE

After the ideal of aggressive wartime masculinity had withered, stars like David and Angie Bowie were on the cutting edge of fashion and expression. Angie's bold instinct for costume design early in David's career popularized stage makeup and flashy fabrics for musicians, sparked the birth of the glam rock scene, and blew open the definition of *manly*. By 1971, when this snapshot was taken, draped trousers, cosmetics, sun hats, jumpsuits, and blouses were common in David's wardrobe.

David and Angie were photographed in their home at Haddon Hall wearing dresses. Angie wore a sleeveless, velvet, mod pinafore dress with a striped shirt and Mary Janes. David wore a floral dress open to the navel and tall suede campus boots. Considering the tight fit of the shoulder and the short length of the sleeve, it's possible that David's outfit was borrowed from Angie's closet or purchased from a women's boutique. Their hair was nearly identical, parted to the left and below the shoulder.

Interestingly, the Haddon Hall photographs were taken before Bowie's career really took off. A gardener owned their home, which sat in a quaint neighborhood in Kent, England, and several members of Bowie's band lived there with them, along with a cat named Satan and the couple's newborn son, Zowie. But their daily lives and music were anything but suburban; both challenged the mainstream with gender fluidity.

David Bowie and wife Angie photographed at their home on April 20, 1971.

WE ARE ALL WOMEN UNDERNEATH

Around the same time that David Bowie and his wife were experimenting with genderfluid dress swapping, lesbian magazine *The Ladder* was running articles on controversial shifts in American culture. This short essay from the November 1964 issue was emphatic that women consider pants as not only a practical option but an empowering one. The next series of images explore how pants and skirts became so gendered, and how the wall between male and female fashion in the West began crumbling.

The Ladder, November 1964, Archives Center, National Museum of American History.

focus on fashion

Pants are proper! The running debate among top fashion designers on both sides of the Atlantic has at last subsided. With help from HARPER'S, VOGUE, and the NEW YORK TIMES, the ayes have it! This season you can wear pants absolutely anywhere - which means dandy pants for town and fancy pants for evening. You can choose from knickers, britches, jumpsuits, pantsuits, pant-shifts, etc. Combine with a champion-swimmer hairdo sleeked back behind your ears and a cropped coat. An inside contact reports that fashion artists are being told to draw their panted women to "look like lesbians." But who can be sure what that means?

Let's review what fashion experts were saying about pants. "Enough women wear pants now - mentally, I mean" (Geoffrey Beene). "I've worn pants for years and they are <u>not</u> comfortable" (Nando Sarmi). "I adore them. It's a way of life I understand" (Eloise Curtis). "Enough is enough... Pants are not yet for 21' or the Automat" (Anne Klein). "It's such a definitive fashion statement" (Stanley Herman). "There is not enough variety of sizes to accomodate all our little derrieres" (Trigere). Mrs. Vreeland of VOGUE sidestepped the whole controversy: "No matter what a woman wears she's always a woman.... My dear, we are all women underneath."

+ + + + + + + +

The Sunday, Sept. 20th N. Y. TIMES explored the His-is-Hers trend. They quote fashion philosopher James Laver: "Emancipation of women must ultimately mean the emergence of a matriarchal society. In such as age, male and female costume will invariably come so close as to be nearly identical." In the same article, Debbie Turbeville of HARPER'S BAZAAR declares: "There is a chic about women wearing men's clothes. ... A really independent woman should be able to get her clothes anywhere. Why does it have to be a woman's shop?"

+ + + + + + + +

What every lesbian knows about the status of women in our society was discussed with sensitivity by Paul Johnson, writing in the English magazine NEW STATESMAN for July 24, 1964. Mr. Johnson explains that "fundamental issues of human freedom" - for women - lie behind the topless dress controversy. He notes that the topless dress began as a gimmick intended to make the low-cut gown seem less daring, therefore more tempting, to the inhibited buyer. The press went along with the gimmick for the sake of lively copy. Then to the astonishment of designers, topless dresses actually began to sell well in the stores where they were available. Consequently, new social and moral questions have to be faced squarely.

16

Mr. Johnson, who did research on the subject, says a majority of the women wearing the topless dresses are "perfectly ordinary housewives and working girls...." Yet officials (all male and all in offices geared to defending the status quo) line up to denounce a man to denounce such exposure. For example, the prosecuting counsel in a case in California, speaking of a pretty girl who had worn a topless bathing suit, accused the girl of "throwing filth in the faces of the police and the public." Nudists, strip-tease artists, and call girls also hate the topless trend for the threat it poses to their special monopolies. Test cases are reportedly being contrived.

But, Mr. Johnson points out, if such exposure be a crime of indecency, then it is so because of the view that women's breasts are obscene. We admire the philosophical level to which Mr. Johnson carries the controversy: "The obscenity, if any exists, must and can only lie in the eyes of the beholder. What the law is in fact saying is that women must not expose their breasts because men are obscene. And here we come to the heart of the matter. The law is made by men and for men; the woman is, as it were, incidental to it. She is regarded more in the nature of an instrument, an impersonal property, without legal conscience of her own, whose significance consists solely in the way men react to her.... The interests of the woman are rejected as irrelevant. The law, being entirely masculine in orientation, cannot conceive that a woman may wish to show her breasts without any other motive than that she is proud of them.... Here...we have a very simple and straightforward issue of personal liberty, which goes straight to the heart of the continued subjection and subordination of women in our society.... Women have got the vote and much else of the formal impedimenta of equality; they have yet to break through the social mould which still treats them as objects rather than persons. A silly season stunt - or a revolt of the still-inferior sex?"

Since you put it that way, Mr. Johnson, we're almost tempted to buy a topless dress tomorrow.

– Melanie

SPECIAL NOTICES

- THE LADDER does not subscribe to a news clipping service. We get ours fresh from the field! <u>You</u> are our only source. Next time you see a news item that might interest LADDER readers, won't you pluck it for us? Please give date and name of publication. Dispatch to the Editor, c/o DOB.

- WHEN YOU MOVE, please notify our Circulation Manager. The postage rate used for THE LADDER does <u>not</u> permit forwarding even though your former post office may have your new address. Avoid missing any issues! Send your new address promptly to the Circulation Manager in San Francisco.

17

PANTALETTE SUFFRAGETTE
WHO WEARS THE PANTS?

Women in the West have struggled for the right to wear the pants (literally and physically) for more than three hundred years. If the binary means we can't have male without female, then trousers for men and skirts for women are the sartorial symbols of gendered life. The trouser symbolized a tool for work, war, and sports—active, outdoorsy, and practical. The skirt was seen as passive, impractical (think extremely wide hoop skirts and constrictive pencil skirts), and for staying indoors.

In tandem with a craze for exercise, bicycling, and open-air pursuits, the suffragette movement in America and England was ramping up as Amelia Bloomer introduced her revolutionary new female trousers (nicknamed "bloomers") in 1851. The need for clothes that women could move in tilted "sporting" dress more toward the typically masculine trouser: full, ankle-length, skirt-like trousers and knee-length skirts with "bloomers" underneath. Once the freedom of trousers started creeping into women's closets, there was no going back.

But it was not an easy path, and imagery around suffrage was cleverly deceptive. The 1909 Dunston-Weiler Lithographic Co. postcard on page 92 portrays an endearing, coy young woman wearing a pair of blue dungarees, white "shirtwaist" blouse, and exaggerated, fashionably oversized hat. Communications and gender studies scholar Catherine Helen Palczewski has collected hundreds of these popular postcards, including the twelve-card series containing this "Pantalette Suffragette," which also featured gender- swapping illustrations like a man in an apron doing laundry next to a baby on the floor and a woman police officer in trousers holding a rolling pin.[6] The visual imagery of the suffragette focuses on the controversial fashion—a woman in trousers—but the subtext was that society was in danger: if women got the vote, moral decay would follow.

In Victorian society, women's liberation threatened to topple the orderly gendered social structure America and England were used to (England's Queen Victoria being the exception). Men's and women's roles would be remixed and reversed, women would take men's jobs and lose interest in children and the household, and men would be forced to step into women's roles.[7]

This 1909 American postcard titled "Pantalette Suffragette, in the sweet bye and bye" illustrates through caricature how uncomfortable Victorian society was with female power and authority.

PEACOCKS TO PENGUINS

During and after the French Revolution, fashion trends fluctuated wildly for both binary genders. In the early-nineteenth-century illustration by Thomas-François Guérin of "Fashion and Its Development" on page 95, we see the stark sartorial difference between the Regency man in his tight buckskin breeches, cropped coat, and high cravat and the new metropolitan Industrial Revolution man, wearing wide, ultra-high-waisted, balloon-shaped trousers and mutton frock-coat sleeves. In the background, soldiers left over from multiple European wars are dressed in tight trousers. I spoke with dress historian, academic, and menswear guru Chloe Chapin about men's fashion at the time, when the Industrial Revolution pushed men further away from self-expression through fashion, while it pushed women further toward fashion as a symbol of frivolity.

Benda: Chloe, your current research focuses on menswear and the gendered binary of the Western fashion system. How does menswear change through European history, and what does that tell us about men, gender identity, and gender roles?

Chapin: I agree that my work on men's suits is rooted in binaries. It's just that what the binary is changes. Because before what [British psychologist John Carl] Flügel called "the great masculine renunciation,"[8] which occurred at the end of the eighteenth century, the main binary in dress was between rich people and poor people.

Then men adopted plain, uniform suits, and the whole system of fashion changed. Suddenly, the same markers of impracticality that once signaled the upper classes were newly associated with women's fashion, and practicality was associated with men's clothing. I call this shift in men's fashion "peacocks to penguins," but it affected more than just masculine style—it also harnessed the idea of fashion to both femininity and frivolity, while men's suits were associated with equality and democracy.

I see suits as gendered power hiding in plain sight, which we can't see because of their plainness and uniformity. But another argument that I'm trying to make is that suits also harmed white men. It affected them in a different way than women or nonwhite, non-Western, or nonheteronormative people, because they held more power. But rejecting fashion cut white men off from the full range of humanity that you have access to when you're allowed to be decorative and beautiful. It cut them off from a full range of textiles and adornment, from wearing color, pattern, and texture, from wearing nail polish and dangly earrings and swishy skirts. I like to call suits the armor and straitjacket of masculinity.

Benda: In the Western world, masculinity typically represents power and dominance. How do pants, trousers, and bifurcated garments reflect this?

Chapin: You can look at pants through the lens of practicality—it's easiest to climb trees or ride a horse wearing pants. But the history of pants is also entangled in class, because in the eighteenth century, trousers were worn by sailors and agricultural workers (including enslaved people). Instead of wearing trousers, gentlemen wore knee breeches and silk stockings until the 1820s, when trousers were adopted as elite fashion.

Benda: How did the progression of breeches to trousers change the male image? And how did the nineteenth-century evolution of trousers for both men and women manifest differently for the two binary identities?

Chapin: Fashionable trousers are an interesting phenomenon. For decades around the turn of the nineteenth century, fashionable men wore very tight, form-fitting buckskin breeches, which accentuated both the thighs and the genitals. When trousers were adopted in the next decades, they were made of dark wool that sheathed a man from the waist to the floor. Then men covered themselves even more by wearing frock coats, which had skirts that fell to the knee. In this way, men were essentially desexed through the introduction of the trousers. I should clarify when I say desexed—it's more of an illusion of being desexed. Men's sexuality didn't go away, it was just hidden.

For women, you have this fashionable uptake in trousers in the 1920s and 1930s, when postwar women had stopped wearing corsets, they were smoking, they were driving. A lot of that came out of women entering the workforce in WWI and getting the right to vote. Women were getting a taste of different kinds of freedom, meaning they were leaving the house and entering the workforce. They were postponing marriage and raising children, because all the men were off fighting in the war. These two examples show how fashion doesn't happen outside of culture. Fashion is a mirror of culture, but it's also a driver of culture.

BENDING THE RULES: FASHION BEYOND THE BINARY

"Fashion and its Developement," an early-nineteenth-century engraving captioned from the point of view of a daughter and wife: "Our Fathers. Our Husbands. Which is the most absurd?"

REGENCY DRESS
NEOCLASSICAL DIVISIONS

In early 1800s Regency England and Post-Revolutionary France, women were traditionally seen as precariously delicate, symbolized by their garments in light pastels, frothy cottons, and fine silks. Men, however, were seen as rough by nature and wore dark tones, woolen fabrics, and leather to complement their temperament. Western Europe became obsessed with the idea of natural order in defining its new social and political ideals. By making sex and gender the same according to nature, the West created a rigid fashion dichotomy.

Gone were the floral motifs, pastels, and lace that had previously been acceptable in men's clothing. Men were now seen as arbiters of order, reason, and the state. They were valued for their sacrifices more than their contributions, expected to martyr themselves for society. As such, playfulness and invention were no longer part of mainstream masculine fashion in the West by the early 1800s, replaced by sobriety and militarism. The feminine was also regulated through these new gender boundaries and the notion of a natural order. The proportions of Regency dresses even mirrored those of infant baptismal gowns, suggesting a woman's submission to God, father, and husband.

OPPOSITE LEFT
This 1830s dress is made of delicate, cream-colored cotton and has a sloped neckline that softens the shoulder into submission compared with the proud posture of masculine tailoring. The high waist suggests an adolescent figure, and the wearer's cleavage was separated by a two-inch-wide bust "divorcer" that neutralized a full bosom.

OPPOSITE RIGHT
This Italian men's tailcoat ensemble from 1830—tailored from solid black wool with flat brass buttons that expand across the chest, giving the look an air of authority—perfectly expresses the times. It's paired with a black silk stock fastened around the neck and black kid gloves.

"The clothing of women must have a sex;
and this costume must contrast with ours.
A woman must be a woman from her head
to her toes."[9]

STILETTOS

Though stacked heels of leather or wood were first worn by men in the late 1500s to show off their athletic calf muscles, the twentieth-century stiletto for women was made possible by new steel rod technology. Heels could reach five inches and higher, and foot deformities from wearing stilettos could make it impossible for a woman to walk in flat-soled shoes again.

YET THEY SAY WOMEN ARE MAKING GREAT STRIDES.

(IM) MOBILITY

Western dress is punctuated by fashion encoding women's restriction and enabling men's freedom. Here are five of the most notorious immobilizing fashions for women and six of the most adventurous fashions for men. The twentieth-century switch-up of women in denim jeans and motorcycle jackets and men in stilettos and voluminous skirts is a breath of fresh air, but most of Western fashion history (and society) wanted the opposite: for the binary genders to follow the rules.

HOBBLE SKIRT

One of fashion's least practical garments, the hobble skirt, was unsurprisingly short-lived. It came into fashion in 1908 and disappeared when WWI started in 1914. The skirt featured fetters or "leg irons" to keep a woman from walking with a normal stride. Fashion designer Paul Poiret took credit for hobbling women and said, "Yes, I freed the bust, but I shackled the legs."[10]

LOTUS SHOES

Beginning in the Song dynasty in 960 CE, small feet were all the rage in China and remained so until the early twentieth century. Achieving that delicate footprint required girls to bind and break their feet to fit into tiny, narrow, lotus shoes. This led women to have lifelong pain when walking and ensured they remained close to home.

CAGES

Whether a set of panniers, a hoop skirt, or a bustle, skirt structures invented between 1700 and 1900 restricted women's ability to walk, sit, or even fit through doors. Because the design of fashion—not to be confused with the construction of clothing, which was primarily women's work—was considered to be a man's vocation until the early twentieth century, we can safely assume that all of these structures were designed by men for women.

OFF-THE-SHOULDER BODICES

The dropped armhole on an 1860s bodice from the American Civil War days of *Gone with the Wind* was lower than the ball of the shoulder, making it impossible for women to lift their arms above their heads.

FLIGHT SUIT

Early airplanes made robust, padded-leather flight suits—like this one worn by a Tuskegee airman in 1945—crucial survival tools. Photographs of men at war and in action splashed across newspapers, and the precursor to the jumpsuit was born.

SAFARI LOOK

The British colonization of India beginning in 1858 gave birth to the four-pocket, desert-hued safari suit, complete with pith helmet. Made in lightweight cotton fabric for withstanding heat and belted at the waist, the look embodied exotic travel to faraway places for troops leaving the rainy British Isles.

MOTORCYCLE JACKET

Dangerous twentieth-century sports like motorcycling and car racing meant that leather jackets with reinforced shoulders and elbows became the sexiest fashion choice for men who wanted to look adventurous (but didn't necessarily have to face danger!).

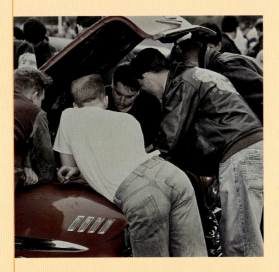

DENIM JEANS

Eighteenth-century French blue workwear fabrics made their way to America on the backs of traders and tailors. Denim was made into dungarees, jeans, and coveralls as gold miners, railroad workers, and loggers needed practical gear for exploration and plunder.

RIDING BOOTS

Originating in Persia in the tenth century CE, the heeled horse-riding boot was designed to stay in stirrups as men galloped adventurously across the land. The heel made its way to royal courts from Elizabethan times onward, then into men's fashion (as often happens with military dress).

BACKPACK

Found in a melting glacier on the border of Austria and Italy on Ötzi the Iceman, a mummified hunter, the earliest frame backpack is five thousand years old. Much later, from the late 1800s up until today, hikers and military troops refined the backpack into the ultimate mobile accessory, like the one shown here from WWII. Hikers, bikers, workers, explorers, and archaeologists soon filled their packs and set off for adventure, turning the backpack into a fashion favorite.

THE HWAROT
SEXUAL SYMPATHETIC MAGIC

Like the post–French Revolution binary framework that helped structure a new order and sort men and women into social roles in the West, a similar framework exists across countries with Confucian roots. Confucianism is a moral and ethical code developed in the sixth century BCE by Kongfuzi, with a philosophy that focused on the ebb and flow of harmony, both in nature and in society.

In second-century BCE China, the newly unified Han dynasty was in a precarious position of power and facing constant challenge. To unify the country under the emperor, court philosopher Dong Zhongshu reinterpreted early Confucianism to serve the state and redefined the relationship between male and female fashion. What Confucius had called *harmony*, Dong redefined as *balance*, thus making yin and yang a hierarchy.[11] Balance, after all, does not require both powers to be equal and fluid.

According to Dong, there are three major yin and yang relationships in society that are imperative to order: the ruler and his minister, the father and his son, and the husband and his wife. Yang is the ruler, the father, and the husband. It is the sun, light, humanity, and benevolence. Yin is the minister, the son, and the wife, defined by the moon, shade, emotion, and greed.

In countries with Confucian roots, it is customary for women (of the moon) to wear

warm hues and men (of the sun) to wear cool hues to balance out their natures. This hwarot is the bridal robe of Princess Bogon of the Korean Joseon dynasty. She wore it at the age of thirteen for her wedding in 1830. It is lined in blue silk for a woman's inner nature and has a red silk exterior that represents her duties and how yang (or her husband) will guide her in her marriage. From butterflies to peonies to ducks, every stitch of embroidery is symbolic of matrimonial harmony, fertility, longevity, and fortune.[12]

BENDING THE RULES: FASHION BEYOND THE BINARY

Princess Bogon's nineteenth-century "Hwarot," or bridal robe, in the collection of the National Palace Museum of Korea.

THE MODERN DIVIDE

On a hot day in July 1853, US Commodore Matthew C. Perry weighed anchor in Tokyo Bay intending to intimidate Japan to open trade with the West. He succeeded: by 1868, Japan's isolationist "Sakoku" policy was abolished, and the rise of the Meiji period began as global trade flooded in, bringing Western fashion. Starting in 1871, the Meiji government began allowing men to cut their hair short in the Western style, eventually cutting off topknots by force. But women were punished if they cut their hair without permission from their local government.

This black-and-white photograph of a family group shows this binary divide. The woman wears a printed kimono, while two of the men wear modern Western 1920s suits with characteristically strong shoulders, narrow waists, and wide trousers. While the woman's hair is long and styled in a traditional Japanese fashion, the men have the neat, cropped short hair typically worn with a Western suit of the time.

While Japanese men were forced to be soldiers of progress, marching into a modern era in connection with the rest of the industrialized world, Japanese women were forced to be the keepers of tradition. This is a phenomenon seen in many nations across Asia in the twentieth century, in which business and politics were conducted by men wearing Western three-piece suits. This visual split between the roles of men and women in society enforced an era defined by the Western binary.

SAKOKU

The "locked country" policy that separated Japan from the West from 1608 to 1868, Sakoku limited the cultural impact of Spanish and Portuguese missionaries to Japan.

Twentieth-century portrait of three young Japanese men: one man in traditional Japanese clothing and two in Western-style business suits, and a woman wearing a traditional Japanese kimono.

RED CARPET ROYALTY
WHO WEARS THE SKIRTS?

Brad Pitt, Timothée Chalamet, and Jared Leto are all red-carpet royalty, usually seen in trouser-based tuxes, suits, or sharp separates. In the past few years, though, all of them have broken the Western binary by wearing skirts on press tours or at awards events. Why is the West so slow to catch up to skirts for men if much of the globe has been wearing them for millennia?

Historically, Western fashion toyed with the idea of skirt-adjacent men's fashions like pumpkin breeches (ultrawide, knee-length breeches) and the houppelande (originally a long pleated, belted outer garment lined with fur). The houppelande became shorter and shorter, until, by the 1490s, it was essentially a miniskirt, worn with thick, form-fitting woolen leggings.

Around the world, various names for skirts for men—kilt (Scotland), lungi (India), sarong (Indonesia), fustanella (Greece), and sulu (Fiji)—attest to their popularity. But in the West, as Chloe Chapin noted earlier, power and authority have generally been conveyed through wearing trousers. Putting on a skirt in the West says something different than putting one on in Saudi Arabia, for instance. Saudi Arabian men wear a version of the skirt in plaid or plain fabrics and go shirtless to beat the heat, while the Saudi robe, a long white cotton garment called the thobe, and the shemagh head covering (anchored with a black cord egal), are the national dress for men.

"A man does not wear his masculinity on his clothes; his virility is in his head."[13] That's how "l'enfant terrible" couture genius Jean Paul Gaultier defined his 1985 collection introducing beautifully draped skirt suits for men. If a skirt meant femininity in the West at the time, and femininity was the opposite of masculinity, a Western-style skirt was off-limits to men. Fashion journalists were divided, exclaiming that Gaultier's runway show was outrageous, risqué, groundbreaking, and revolting. Gaultier himself didn't think it was controversial, since he wore kilt-like skirts himself and global dress for men often included variations on skirt shapes.[14]

Elizabeth Hawes, an American fashion designer, wrote the rebellious book *Fashion Is Spinach* in 1938 and titled one of the chapters "Men Might Like Skirts." Hawes designed new fashions for the early USSR and pondered the question of why early twentieth-century men continued wearing uncomfortable, restrictive fashion:

> God help the American male with his background of having to be Masculine. It's practically as all-pervading in his conscious and subconscious as the fashionable lady's desire to be fashionable. In 1935 it was not masculine to wear shirts open at the neck; it was not masculine to wear colors except navy, black, brown, gray, and tan.[15]

BELOW
BELOW
Western men's fashion accelerated throughout the fifteenth century, culminating in a belted short jerkin (or early doublet) with a peplum mimicking a micro-skirt. As seen in this 1482–1485 illuminated manuscript of Florentines fleeing the Black Plague, women's skirts stayed floor length and continued to do so until four hundred years later.

RIGHT
Brad Pitt chose an espresso-colored linen skirt suit from fashion designer Haans Nicholas Mott for his appearance at a 2022 *Bullet Train* film screening in Germany.

What Gaultier and Hawes are pointing out is that the fuss about men's skirts is cultural, not functional. It's about letting go of rules and expectations so everyone can enjoy playing with fashion.

WHO WEARS THE KILTS?

Around the world many men wear skirts in vibrant hues and patterns, from plaid lungis to multicolored kilts. The following chart looks at how the phenomenon of tartan textiles developed and why a kilt was worn only by men.

1745 CE

Tartan became a Scottish national patriotic symbol during the Jacobite rebellion against English rule. Insurgent leader Bonnie Prince Charles advanced on the English leading kilt-wearing regiments. In defeat, he retreated to the Scottish Highlands wearing this tartan suit with velvet cuffs. After the English crushed the Jacobites, they banned tartan with the Diskilting Act. This showed how powerful the textile was as a national symbol of Scotland. Charles went into exile, and his coat eventually entered the collection of the National Museum of Scotland archives, where it remains today.

240 CE

It all started with a multicolor crisscross weave: plaid. Found on top of ancient Roman coins bearing the mark of Roman emperor Severus Alexander, this fragment of undyed, chevron-woven cloth is one of the earliest known plaids. Everyone could wear plaid; gender restrictions didn't apply...yet.

SIXTEENTH CENTURY CE

Preserved by a peatbog in Glen Affric in the Scottish Highlands, the earliest-known tartan fragment shows a distinctive orange, brown, green, and red pattern. Tartan is plaid but infused with cultural meaning and clan association.

EARLY EIGHTEENTH CENTURY

The kilt is born! But only for men, especially military men. Up to eighteen feet of plaid fabric was hand-pleated and pinned down each time it was folded around the body. Proving too cumbersome and time-consuming for everyday use, the "great kilt" became ceremonial. The "little kilt" used less fabric and was pleated and sewn in advance.

LE PRÉTEXTE

1815 CE

After Napoleon's empire collapsed, Paris was overrun by foreign troops. The French worried that the sight of sexy, manly, militarized Scottish legs in kilts would cause scandal among respectable women.

1822 CE

Recently crowned King George IV visited Scotland to establish his rule and commissioned a full suit of highland dress for the occasion. Fashionable society men wore "kilt suits" to a ball in his honor. Women were asked to refrain from wearing too much tartan so the men could shine.

1995 CE

Iconic English fashion designer Vivienne Westwood wove Scottish tartan—a textile born of rebellion—through many of her collections. This men's suit from the collection of the National Museums Scotland features the Bruce of Kinnaird tartan made by longtime collaborator Lochcarron of Scotland. Alexander McQueen spun Westwood's tartan into a complex historical commentary with his 1995 Highland Rape collection. Referencing Scottish portraiture, the collection explored England's domination (rape) of Scotland. McQueen created tortured, twisted garments featuring tartan for women. Can a woman truly wear a kilt? Historically, no—women wore tartan as skirts. But in the spirit of Westwood and McQueen and Scottish rebellion? Yes!

1782 CE

After intense lobbying, the ban was repealed and tartan continued to define Scottish identity. *Invented tradition* describes how Scottish nobility then created bespoke clan tartans to immortalize their heritage. Highland dress meant a matching jacket, trews (close-cut, short drawers), and the plaid (made from a length of precisely pleated tartan).

(SINGULAR)

"Cause boy it's cool if
you got blue.
We got the pink."[1]

—Janelle Monáe

ingular identities lie at the ends of the spectrum: no gray area, no nuance. They are hypermasculine or hyperfeminine, either by choice or through the pressures of society. In this section, a mix of Western and Eastern cultural imagery tells the story of these gendered signifiers and how they can influence an individual's presentation and self-expression. The military, police forces, super-heroes, and cowboys exemplify traditionally male presentation, while Barbie, *Playboy*, and the restrictions of fashion (corsets, crinolines, bustiers, and bras) typify traditionally female presentation.

But looking at an identity's opposite can be illuminating, as it reveals our thoughts about the original. Several of the images in this chapter show how people have reclaimed heteronormative imagery for their own authentic gender. Two contemporary individuals who use fashion to celebrate who they truly are both identify as a singular identity, but surprisingly not a traditional one. Olympic medalist Caster Semenya emphatically identifies as a woman, despite intense media attention about her perceived "nonfeminine" appearance. Fashion model and engineer Mark Bryan strongly identifies as a man, despite surprising the world (and Instagram) with his pencil skirt and heel combos.

Subverting masculine and feminine identities with clothing forms a large part of this section: American women in WWII workwear take over men's roles as soldiers go off to war, gay rodeo riders claim a traditionally heterosexual ritual, a genderfluid man appears on the cover of *Playboy* magazine, and an empowered, autonomous Barbie is envisioned "off-camera."

Across this section, childhood plays a key role. As children, our gender influences depend on where we are born and into what social class, who our parents are, and what schools we go to. School and sports uniforms are some of the first uniforms we wear, and we learn through them to conform, unify, disguise, and belong.

The classic men's suit—both how it is used to show power, authority, and compliance and how it can be subverted—is the first point of exploration. Military dress for men, women, and LGBTQ+ individuals is next, followed by the mythical Wild West. On the feminine side, this section delves into the female silhouette, exemplified by *Playboy* and Barbie imagery, and investigates how women's bodies are traditionally divided into erogenous zones. Finally, two charts contrast how we've worn codpieces and bras as hyper-gendered garments.

Janelle Monáe, music video still and song lyrics, "PYNK," from the 2018 album *Dirty Computer*. Directed by Emma Westenberg, trousers by Duran Lantink, styled by Alexandra Mandelkorn.

WEAR WHAT YOU WANT TO WEAR

Mark Bryan is a sixty-two-year-old, Texas-born engineer based in Germany; a dad, grandfather, and husband; a Porsche enthusiast and football coach. What he is not is gender ambiguous: "I'm very clear what my gender is," he says. "I'm very clear that I'm a man, I just choose basically what I want to wear, and right now, for the last few years, it's been wearing a skirt and high heels."[2] Bryan's almost six hundred thousand Instagram followers tune in for videos of him repairing his Porsche in black stiletto ankle boots and denim pencil skirt or updates on his latest magazine editorial shoot. An interview with Bryan revealed more about his collection of 150 pairs of heels, his newfound fame as a fashion model, and the many assumptions people make about him through his clothes.

Benda: What do the younger generations think of your style?

Bryan: If you look at the demographic on my Instagram, the biggest age range that follows me is twenty-four to thirty-four years old, and sixteen to twenty-four is the second biggest. I have a very young following. I'm old enough to remember when girls couldn't wear pants (until I was in the seventh grade), so that would have been 1969 or the early 1970s. I don't feel any different if I'm wearing pants or wearing a skirt. For me, I'm the same person—it's just an article of clothing.

Benda: What are the reactions to you in the street in Germany versus America because of what you wear?

Bryan: I think me doing this in Germany has made it a lot easier, but I think one of the reasons it's easier is that I still present myself as a very masculine person. People think, "Well he's different, that's a guy wearing a skirt and high heels." I do get the same reactions in Utah or Texas; it just depends on what neighborhood I'm in. In the German town where I live, people are used to me now. I've been in enough German newspapers and TV shows that everyone knows who "Mark the guy who wears a skirt and high heels" is. I go to a restaurant and people no longer stare.

Benda: When you think about fashion and gender identity, what would be your hopes for the future, or what would you like to see more of?

Bryan: My goal is for everyone to be able to wear what they want to wear, without being stereotyped or your gender expression questioned, or more importantly your sexual orientation questioned. My biggest hope is for people to not judge someone's sexual orientation by what they wear. And not just what men wear—it's women too. Eighty percent of my followers are women. A lot of women follow me because they like to wear men's clothes but are afraid of being labeled butch or lesbian. What I'd really like

to accomplish, or I'd like to see in the next twenty years, is for people to have the freedom to wear what they want to wear without fear of being put in a box. And that the clothing stores aren't divided by women or men. Maybe I'm part of that movement to get that thinking going.

Mark Bryan modeling a shirt and tie by Dior Men, vest by Ernest W. Baker, skirt by Marni, gloves and bag by Hermès, and shoes by Amina Muaddi. Styled by Dogukan Nesanir for *Interview*, 2021.

CASTER SEMENYA
HER OWN WOMAN

Early in her childhood, Caster Semenya had an innate love for running. She would chase her siblings down dusty roads in rural, northernmost South Africa. Her subsequent Olympic running career in the 2010s was fraught with controversy and legal battles about her biological gender, but she has always been clear that she identifies as a woman, regardless of European labels. Semenya expresses her vision of womanhood in sports with radiant confidence and clarity, and in 2023 released her memoir, *The Race to Be Myself*.

Her public appearances are elevated by a vibrant collection of looks: black mesh corsets, crisp white tees, and boxy denim jackets, tuxedo dress shirts, and gold bangles. Semenya often wears bespoke suits from South African tailor Row-G. In this image, Semenya's suit from Lezanne Viviers—a Johannesburg-based designer of "genderless" clothing—is a delicious blend of assumptions about both male and female style. Its extra-wide shoulders hearken back to zoot suits worn by young Black men in Harlem, New York, in the 1930s, while the pink tufted tweed softens its presentation. Semenya is now a style icon in Africa, sometimes seen on the fashion runway and often on the red carpet.

"I'm an African, I'm a woman, I'm a different woman."[5]

Caster Semenya, wearing a suit by Viviers and sandals by Europa Art. Photographed by Alice Mann for the *Guardian* newspaper, October 28, 2023.

WOMEN'S WORK

Award-winning veteran war correspondent Kate Adie learned the power of uniform early on in English elementary school. As she writes in her 2003 book *Corsets to Camouflage: Women and War*, stiff, uncomfortable school uniforms had "one good aspect: absolutely no decisions to be made in the morning." She continues, "So at a very early age, I'd sampled the impact of uniforms: their power to deliver an instantaneous message, their ability to reduce the individual to a unit, simultaneously marking you out and blending you in."[4]

During WWII in England, newly recruited women were surprised when issued men's pajamas instead of women's ones. Some uniforms were designed and manufactured only for men, often leaving women to wear men's surplus coveralls, dungarees, work jackets, and gloves. The 1944 US Army poster "Soldiers without Guns" shows three ways women could pitch in during WWII: as an office typist, a welder, or a factory worker. The typist wears typical feminine fashion but the welder wears a plaid flannel shirt, thick brown leather belt, and dungarees, while the factory worker wears blue coveralls with a white shirt, red patterned kerchief, and work gloves—garments seen on ranchers, cowboys, and farmers at the time.

Even civilian women sometimes wore fashionable (but not practical) versions of their husband's uniforms, like this India Campaign tunic. This 1880s navy wool bodice with black military braid in the National Museums of Ireland archives has a matching floor-length wool skirt, which would have been underpinned by layers of petticoats and a woven cane bustle and pointed, heeled, lace-up boots.

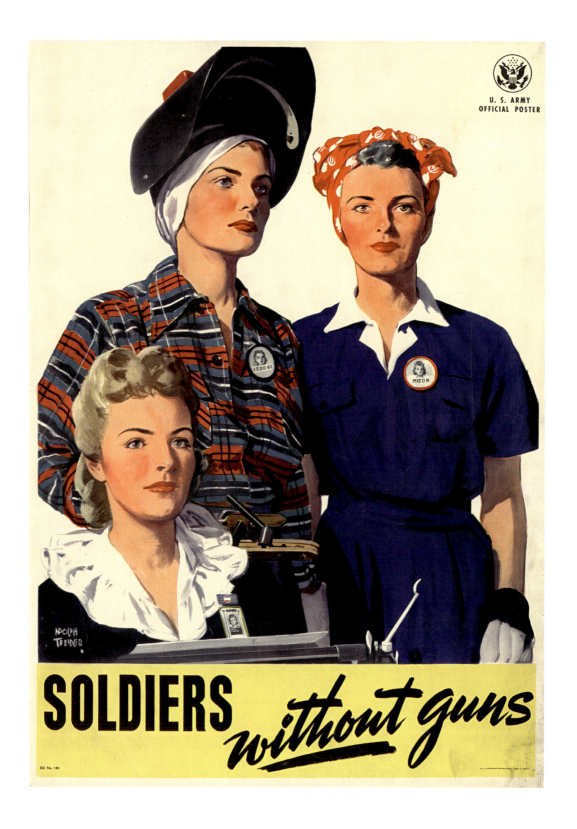

Motor Corps
of America

OPPOSITE

A US Government Printing Office poster from 1944 illustrates the roles women could play in the war effort. If it seems frivolous that all of them have perfect brows and red lipstick, it wasn't— a woman's patriotic duty was to remain well-groomed to keep morale high.

ABOVE

Women's military uniforms were historically genderized variants of men's uniforms. In WWI, Women's Motor Corps uniforms like the one in this 1918 poster were a beige-collared shirt, a brown wool necktie, and an olive drab, four-pocket jacket— just like the men's. Instead of trousers, women wore a calf-length, button-through, A-line skirt.

HEROES IN DISGUISE

While Mark Bryan is comfortable taking risks, others like the safety and comfort of following sartorial rules. And all of us have had a moment of feeling like we don't know the rules for formalwear or what to wear for an event. The modern business suit eliminates this problem of how to fit in for traditional men.

Since the Industrial Revolution, the three-piece suit was meant to camouflage and correct any male "flaws," implying that the natural body wasn't up to the task alone. Whatever society deemed unfashionable could be fixed by expert tailoring. Men were expected to be part of the industrial complex, and the suit was the tool they used to conform. As Cally Blackman observes in her book *One Hundred Years of Menswear*, "To adapt a phrase from [architect] Le Corbusier, the suit is a machine for living in, close-fitting but comfortable armor."[5]

In 1957, *Esquire Fashion Guide for All Occasions* was published, hoping to save men from fashion faux pas through witty writing and carefully drawn illustrations. This excerpt suggests that a gentleman could be safe and camouflaged in most social situations in an appropriate suit.

This is the age of the democratic, in which even a king tries to dress like a citizen. A man dresses not to be different but to Belong. Consider the man entering the same cocktail party where the two girls in the identical dresses are glaring at each other.

He is wearing, let us say, an oxford-gray suit. As soon as he enters, he gives a swift glance around at the other men. "Ah," he says to himself, "they're mostly in gray or black. Good—I'm O.K."[6]

It's no coincidence that the gray suit is also Clark Kent's disguise, shown here. The white shirt and dark tie, accented by a sleek quasi-military haircut and the occasional eyeglasses, were already the corporate uniform for businessmen in 1939, when the first stand-alone *Superman* comic was released.

The superhero suit—thanks to post-millennial movies from Marvel, DC Comics, and Disney, as well as to *Star Wars*, *Star Trek*, and *Dune*—wrap the symbolism of military, corporate, and civic uniforms into one neat, expertly designed package. The supersuits feature military-like ingenuity, with sculpted muscle suits under a final decorative layer. In this way the ideal heteronormative male form is essentially layered on top of an actor's body. Like the business suit, the supersuit corrects any unwanted elements. And like police or civic uniforms (and military badges, medals, and patches), a superhero suit is instantly recognizable and carries unique nonverbal branding, graphic design, and logos (the letter *S* on Superman's chest, for instance). Because of these sartorial symbols, traditional Western male roles and imagery stay consistent from battlefields to offices to movie screens.

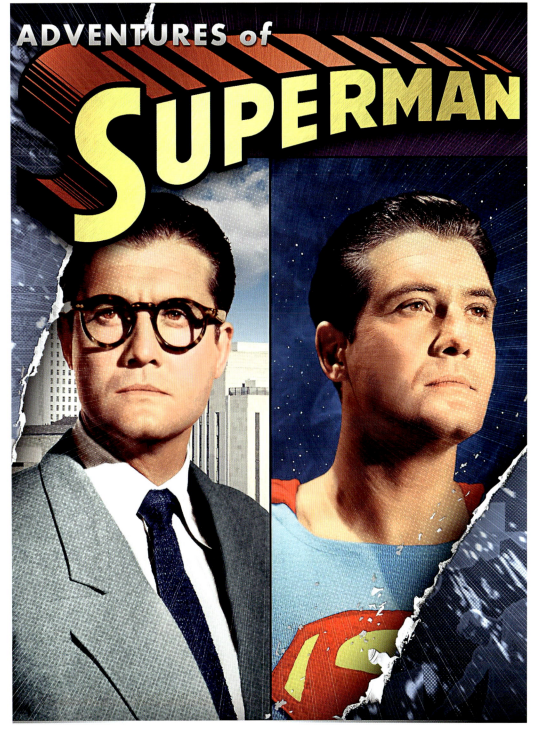

A 1952 poster from *Adventures of Superman* shows actor George Reeves wearing the unobtrusive classic men's gray suit that serves to hide the superhero suit underneath.

This digital rendering of a "salaryman" uses the symbolism of a Western business suit and tie worn with a white-collared pinstripe shirt, camel-colored overcoat, and sleek loafers to illustrate how nonverbal cues telegraph power and status.

SALARYMEN

As Western dress spread internationally during the twentieth century, the modern men's business suit became a badge of industry in Japan. While the feminine role as a symbol of traditional beauty and cultural pride remained largely frozen in time, the masculine role was born of the mindset of a samurai's military sense of self-sacrifice and loyalty, even dying for the cause. (*Karoshi* is the Japanese term for someone who dies by overwork, including by suicide or heart attack.)

Salarymen weren't a new phenomenon, but a continuation of traditional militarism. Thanks to a major economic boom in the 1970s and '80s, the Japanese achieved a fresh chance at globalization and economic domination after the fall of Imperial Japan in 1947. Just like superhero suits, military uniforms, and the samurai's menpo (face armor), the salarymen's Western two-piece suit had a uniformity that erased their personal identities. Only in the details—the brightness of his socks, the width of his shoulder pads in his overcoat, what brand of cigarettes he smoked, or whether his watch was silver or gold—could a man express his personality.[7]

THE SALARYMAN'S GUIDE TO ANONYMOUS POWER

- Choose a somber suit in black or navy blue and ensure your tie is a subdued, patriotic hue.
- Polish your black dress shoes or loafers to a high shine.
- For some flair, match your socks to your tie.
- Consider a camel overcoat with oversized shoulders and lapels that enlarge your silhouette.
- Never, ever stray from the uniform.

TOM OF FINLAND
HIGHWAY PATROL

Legendary erotic illustrator Tom of Finland's subjects were all superheroes. To him, gay men didn't have to be effeminate or take on feminine characteristics. (As a teen in the 1930s, this would have been the only identity available to him as a young gay man.) They could be virile, muscle-bound policemen, soldiers, lumberjacks, dock workers, sailors, and highway patrolmen. As noted in *Dian Hanson: The Little Book of Tom of Finland, Cops & Robbers*, "The uniforms of the California Highway Patrol motorcyclists were his favorite: tan and tight, with high boots and soft black leather gauntlet gloves. He created his own uniform variants as well, a cross between military and civilian police gear, and invented suitably butch criminals for his cops to apprehend."[8]

Tom (born Touko Valio Laaksonen in 1920) had direct experience with military uniforms. He was conscripted as a lieutenant into the Finnish army during WWII (Finland were Axis forces, and Tom would have been persecuted by the Nazis for being gay), where he found an unexpected secret liberation: during bombing blackouts, gay soldiers could find each other in the dark. (At the time, the world wasn't ready for them to be out in the light.) A talented artist, Tom subverted the power of the uniform, harnessed it in his work, and transferred that power to a newly emerging, openly gay community beginning in the 1960s.

"Tom's work must be considered more than just 'dirty drawings' and given some of the credit for the change in the gay world's self-image. When Tom's work was first published, homosexuals thought they had to be imitation women and spent their lives hiding in the shadows. Thirty-five years later, gays were much more likely to be hard-bodied sun-lovers in boots and leather, masculinity personified. From the beginning, he consciously strove to instill in his work a positive, up-beat openness."[9]

Tom of Finland's untitled drawing of two hypermasculine law enforcement officers.

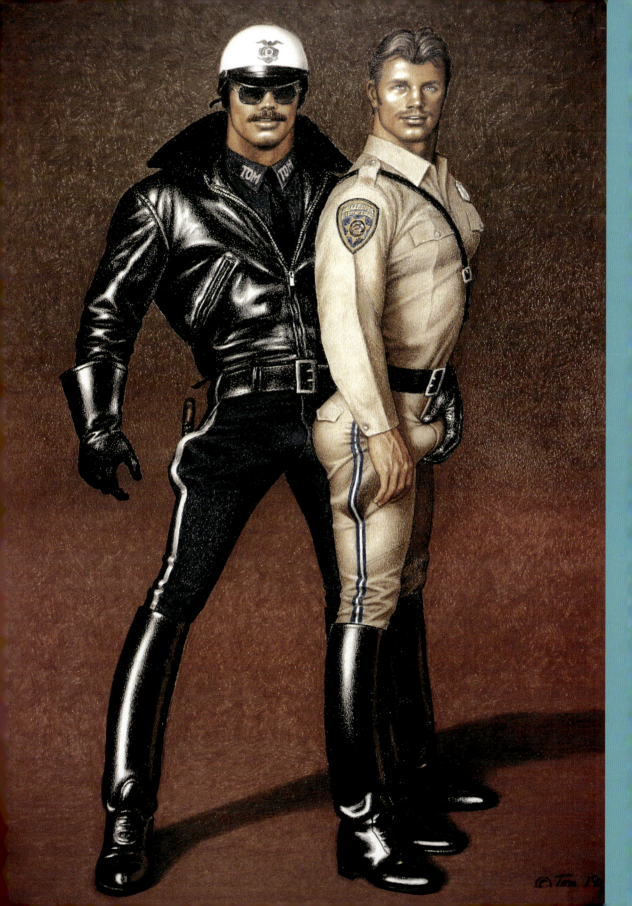

"Sorry Girls......I'm GAY!,"
subversive poster, 1990.

This 1917 Navy recruiting poster shows a sailor in his instantly recognizable navy-blue wool uniform with white trim, riding an orange missile like a bronco, seafoam spraying in the wind. During the gay liberation movement, the chivalrous heteronormative military image was parodied with cheeky interpretations. Like Tom of Finland's work, the 1990 poster in the Smithsonian's collection—a cheerful sailor disappointing the ladies—playfully subverted the heterosexual Navy ensign.

The military uniform is the visual representation of national power, and specifically male power. It can also be part of the closet a heterosexual man can choose from while building his identity. It hangs alongside the Western business suit, the police uniform, and the superhero suit like armor as a universal, accessible, global conveyance. In the 1970s, the Village People included a uniformed army grunt in its roster (which included a cowboy, construction worker, highway patrolman, and motorcycle cop), flipping his hypermasculine identity to a queer version. A uniform means you have joined a club: if you dress like a Marine, you take on the bravery and history of all Marines.

Dress and ceremonial uniforms allow wearers to know where they stand in terms of rank. Badges, sashes, buttons, gold braid, name tags, chevrons, multicolored bars, medals, epaulettes, and emblems are outward signs of status. Uniforms also harness the power of tailoring to "perfect" the male form, meaning that the military could create an army of precisely outfitted soldiers. Dress historian Anne Hollander wrote about the interaction between the male form and representations of power in her seminal book *Sex and Suits*. A suit perfects a man's figure by chiseling away at his natural shape, emphasizing his shoulders, narrowing his waist, lengthening his leg, framing his face, and covering his body in one neutral, harmonious color.

A uniform could elevate a man's status in society and give him a clear role, mirrored by the sailor's uniform. "Join the Navy, the Service for Fighting Men," recruiting poster, 1917.

E. C. "TEDDY BLUE" ABBOTT
COWPUNCHERS

Imagine the strongest, most dashing, flamboyant, and mysterious men arriving in your small 1870s Midwestern town. The myth was that young boys wanted to be them, and all women wanted to marry them. They were the Wild West's first superheroes—cowboys. All elements of cowboy dress point to male virility, from the fitted denim jeans that hearken back to ultra-tight, nineteenth-century, leather military breeches to the leg-lengthening boot heels that echo Persian horse-riding boots. Spurs added a shiny metallic armor accent, the wide-brimmed wool-felted hat gave an aura of the Spanish vaquero mystique from which it came, the American Civil War–style shirt in blood-soaked red referenced military strength, and embroidered leather roping gauntlets had an air of Three Musketeers adventure.

While cowboys now evoke the Old West and might feel old-fashioned, the highly developed aesthetic of their garments is a study in the highest levels of craftsmanship. The design incorporates heritage and storytelling, propelled by a nomadic lifestyle that forced extreme utility—the cowboy look, like military dress, is a perfect balance of form and function. To withstand the rough treatment that came with the job, Western wear had to be made well from quality materials: Stetson was the standard for beautifully made wool hats, saddles and bridles were hand tooled from top-notch leather, and fine hand embroidery reflected Western motifs, telling visual tales of the frontier. Silk or cotton bandanas were visual poems, incorporating traditional motifs from Mexican and Native American iconography. Books like *How the West Was Worn* (2001) and *Cowboys & the Trappings of the Old West* (1997) meticulously detail the history of classic Western films and how cowboy fashion continues to influence rock stars and musicians.[10]

In 1879, "cowpuncher" E. C. "Teddy Blue" Abbott remembered heading home from delivering cattle in Nebraska and stopping to purchase his first store-bought Western gear in the town of North Platte (before that, his mother made all his clothes). "I remember it like it was yesterday. I had a new white Stetson hat that I paid ten dollars for and new pants that cost twelve dollars, and a good shirt and fancy boots. They had colored tops, red and blue, with a half-moon and star on them. Lord, I was proud of these clothes!"[11] So important were these new clothes, Abbott sat for his second-ever photograph in town.

Journalist Helen Huntington Smith interviewed Abbott (then seventy-seven years old) during the winter of 1937, and as he reminisced, she handwrote notes about the dangerous, exhausting, and male-dominated profession of "cowpunching," or cow herding. Throughout the book, he tells of highly gendered roles for frontier men and women: single cowpunchers traveled, worked, visited brothels in towns, and saved their pennies until it was time to meet and marry a respectable young woman.

BENDING THE RULES: FASHION BEYOND THE BINARY

Young women from good families stayed at home on ranches, learning to sew, make clothes, cook, and take care of a household until the right man came along. Abbott remembers his fiancée, Mary, hand making her dark red velvet wedding dress as she waited for him to return from the range.[12]

Women in brothels had more freedom, despite their low status, some refusing to marry and settle down, instead running rooming houses once they aged. Abbott recalls a Miles City, Montana, girl named Connie the Cowboy Queen, whose dress was a visual record of the different cattle brands across Midwestern America: "Connie had a $250 dress embroidered with all the different brands—they said there wasn't an outfit [ranch]…that couldn't find its brand on that dress."[15]

In true Tom-of-Finland style, gay rodeo takes the best of the heteronormative cowboy and subverts it into positive, celebratory, LGBTQ+ pride. In 1976, cowboy Phil Ragsdale organized the first gay rodeo in Nevada, and it spread internationally. The ONE Archives at the University of Southern California, an important collection of LGBTQ+ materials, holds this black-and-white photograph by Scott Greene of two men, arms around each other in a rodeo ring.

KENNETH BAMBERG
THE KOTEKA PROJECT

Finnish photographer Kenneth Bamberg was inspired to explore kotekas, or penis sheaths, after seeing anthropologist Gunnar Landtman's collection from his time in Papua New Guinea in 1910–1912. It made him wonder, "What would I build today of this old symbol of masculinity? So I built my own one and made a photo. I asked some of my friends—classmates, teachers—do you want to build your own for my own tribe in Åland?"[14] Gwyn Conaway interviewed Bamberg in 2024 about his modern take on an ancient phallic symbol.

Bamberg asked a hundred fellow Ålanders, and about twenty—including a philosopher, a parliamentarian, a plumber, a snail farmer, a fisherman, and a postal worker—said yes. He gave them carte blanche to design their own kotekas and choose where they wanted to be photographed. While traditional sheaths are made of dried fruits and gourds for protection from humidity and insects, those of Bamberg's subjects are built with everything from pike fish to seal skins, wife-made socks, pages of the *Phantom* comics, mixtapes, and plumbing pipes. They became a playful exploration of each man's personal identity.

Conaway: What does your own koteka mean to you?

Bamberg: I was sitting outside the sauna, cooling down at my wife's grandma's. I saw this rake and I thought that it was a good way of symbolizing how there are today more different ways of being a man, being a woman, being a human. So these are different roads—different directions you can go in your life. The flowerpot is a basket-like wood, and the metal piece looks like knight's armor, to get a bit of chivalry tied in.

Conaway: The series is so proudly playful. Do you think the men rediscovered boyhood through their kotekas?

Bamberg: Yeah, I had this experience. When I was six or seven I was playing with it. I was putting rubber bands on it. And I remember my grandmother got so furious and screamed at me, "You are never, never, never allowed to do this," and really told me completely off. I was crying a lot. Then when doing this [photo series], it was kind of a liberation. And so [while shooting the series] there was a lot of giggling between us. This reaction happened a few times. It was heartwarming to see this, how much energy and time they put into it.

Kenneth Bamberg's koteka self-portrait from 2014 is among the many photographs he's taken of men and their personalized kotekas.

CODPIECES

Face codpiece, sixteenth century

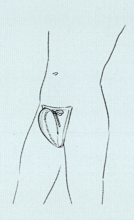

Elizabethan codpiece, sixteenth century

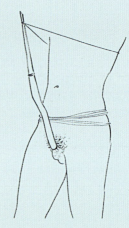

Koteka phallocrypt, Dani people, Papua New Guinea

Animal (F–ck Like a Beast) codpiece, W.A.S.P., 1980s

Gaff panties, 2020s

Merkin, Maison Margiela, 2024

Straw penis sheath, Vanuatu people, Vanuatu Islands

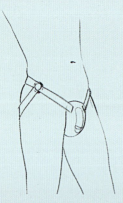

Shape enhancer, 2020s

Sock packing, 2000s

Fundoshi, Japan

GLORIA STEINEM
COLLARS AND CUFFS

Who designed the Playboy bunny costume is a mystery, with multiple theories and as many revisions of the look, but most people recognize it instantly. The core garment, a corseted strapless bodice that came in a rainbow of twelve colors (with dyed-to-match satin bunny ears) accentuates two markers of femininity: the female waist and breasts (more about these shortly). This is finished off with a fluffy white bunny tail pinned on the rear and an iconic marker of women's sexuality, the stiletto heel. Clearly inspired by the Playboy logo, French fashion designer Renée Blot later added the collar and cuffs.[15] The resulting costume couldn't exist without a Western, masculine, business suit to subvert. The white collar is punctuated by a black bow tie, and the cuffs have Playboy bunny cufflinks, referencing menswear minus the shirt and trousers.

Playboy magazine was first published in 1953, with Marilyn Monroe as its centerfold, and the first Playboy Club opened in Chicago in 1960. Three years later, feminist writer and activist Gloria Steinem (seen here serving drinks) went undercover to write a two-part series for *Show* magazine in 1963. Steinem recollects surviving the interviews, costume fittings, fake eyelashes, bosom stuffings, and trainings to start work at the hat check stand.[16] Bunnies were trained to be the ultimate postwar American submissive hostesses, providing all the joys of an attentive "girlfriend" with none of the burdens of a wife and kids. The 1960 *Playboy*

Journalist and feminist icon Gloria Steinem in 1963, posing undercover in her official Playboy bunny costume.

Club Bunny Manual emphasized the importance of perfect behavior, dress, makeup, hair, weight, perfume, punctuality, and teamwork, and even keeping one's cottontail fluffy and white. It detailed how bunnies were required to stay clean: "It is up to each Bunny to make sure that a situation never occurs when she does not have a clean, well-fitting costume, including matching ears and shoes, a clean and fluffy cottontail, immaculate cuffs and collar, proper hose, regulation undergarments, Playboy cuff links, nameplate, and bow tie."[17] Looking pretty was a lot of work! A woman on a *Playboy* cover is so iconic that it has become pop culture shorthand. So what happens when a man ends up on the cover of *Playboy*?

BRETMAN ROCK
A DIVINE BLEND

Bretman Rock was the first gay biologically male *Playboy* cover star, making history in October 2021. All the Playboy bunny symbols—collar, cuffs, ears, tail, corset, heels—are on the cover. Being a *Playboy* cover model is a remarkable milestone, among Rock's many firsts. A first-generation immigrant from the Philippines (now based in Hawai'i), Rock, at age fourteen, was one of the first digital celebrities. Now with nineteen million Instagram followers, Rock spills the tea on genderbending fashion and genderless beauty with a joyous sense of humor (for example, describing his younger self as "Bretman Pebble").

In 2023 Rock wrote *You're That Bitch: & Other Cute Lessons About Being Unapologetically Yourself*, detailing how the *Playboy* photoshoot made Bretman finally feel like a sex symbol.[18] Rock's gay identity and LGBTQ+ advocacy is front and center, but the editorial choice to expose nipples (something a genetically female bunny would have never been able to do on the cover) was revolutionary.

Before *Playboy* stopped publishing nude images in 2015, women's nipples inside the magazine were a main attraction. Free the Nipple campaigns focus on gender equality for all and interrogate why American men can show their nipples in public, but women can't. After legal action, six US states (Utah, Colorado, Wyoming, New Mexico, Kansas, and Oklahoma) can no longer stop a woman from being topless in public and New York City has no laws against toplessness but can arrest women showing their nipple based on notions of public decency and disorder. While Bretman Rock's *Playboy* cover helped in these efforts, maybe it's most important as an aesthetically beautiful commentary on a controversial part of human anatomy.

> **"I identify as a human-fucking-being. I've always been a divine blend of masculine and feminine— so if I look like a lesbian after a bicep-bulging workout, call me he, but if I'm in full makeup wearing a Catholic schoolgirl plaid skirt and barrettes, call me she. I don't mind, I'm cute either way! (Maybe I should just make my own gender at this point . . . . I am a Bretman.)"[19]**

Bretman Rock *Playboy* cover, September 2021.

CORSETS
A MORAL PANIC

As the hypersexualized understructure for not only Playboy bunnies but also Shakespearean heroines, Renaissance damsels in distress, eighteenth-century queens, Victorian wenches, and romance novel cover girls, corsets are one of the most talked-about feminine garments in the history of Western fashion. On one hand, they were demonizing, suggesting women who wore them were impractical and frivolous. On the other, they were a necessity in Western high society, where women were expected to behave and dress according to the status of their household. Always polarizing, corsets gave women no neutral choice: wear one and you're vain, don't wear one and you're a disgrace. Debates raged at the end of nineteenth-century society as the West struggled with the morality of women's dress.

Lampooning the tightrope that women had to walk between society's expectations and everyday discomfort, this caricature shows a fashionable lady cranking a fictional wooden machine that tightens the corset around her companion's waist to dangerously tiny proportions. Corsets had briefly dropped out of fashion from 1800 to 1820, giving women a breather. Post–French Revolution Empire dresses were sheaths

"A Correct View of the New Machine for Winding Up the Ladies," by William Heath, from 1828.

of corset-less white muslin inspired by ancient Greece and Rome, symbolizing revolutionary democratic ideals. From 1830 onward, corsets were back with a vengeance, changing shape each decade to elevate Victorian fashion obsessed with new Industrial Revolution technologies like steel corset boning, vibrant synthetic dyes, and lightweight steel crinolines.

BRAS, BUSTIERS, AND BUST WRAPPERS

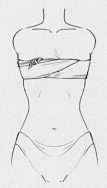

Mamillare, ancient Greece

Chest binder, 2020s

Rope binder, Mucubal people, Angola

Dudou, Qing dynasty, China

Grecian girdle, 1900s

Lengberg bra, fifteenth century

Bust harness, ancient Greece

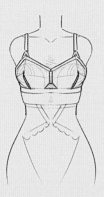

Bullet bra, 1950s

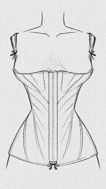

Romantic corset, 1830s

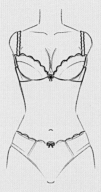

WonderBra, 1980s

Elizabethan stays, seventeenth century

KUSŌZU
THE FEMME FATALE

This eighteenth-century kusōzu painting of a seated noblewoman features a rare and remarkable way of dressing the body. The "junihitoe," a set of twelve multicolored robes precisely layered on top of each other, reflects a thousand-year-old formal court dress tradition. Since the 1400s CE, Japanese artists have used beautiful aristocratic women as corpses in kusōzu paintings, which depict stages of bodily decay after death. "In all the paintings the corpse is unmistakably female," writes scholar Carolyn A. Day. "In life she is seated with flowing black tresses, dressed in twelve-layered court robes."[20] Partly created for Buddhist meditation practices, these paintings would depict the noblewoman's bare breasts or her funerary scene with intimate attention, robes peeled back to expose her body as it decayed.[21] Like the corsets, bustiers, and bras in the previous chart and the couture bust prosthetics in the image on page 140, the kusōzu paintings reinforce the binary fetish society has for women's breasts.

"Kusōzu: the death of a noble lady and the decay of her body. Stage 0: the noble lady in her lifetime," eighteenth-century watercolor.

BENDING THE RULES: FASHION BEYOND THE BINARY

MAISON MARGIELA
THE FASHIONABLE DECAY

Decay, beauty, and death also feature in John Galliano's Maison Margiela 2024 Artisanal Collection. "The collection's synthesis between the painterly process and the ritual of dressing ignites a study of the muse-like relationship formed between artists and their anatomical lay dolls."[22] "It is conveyed in doll-like accents, in the striptease of shirting dresses, and in tweed skirt-suits."[23] Galliano was inspired by French painter Kees van Dongen, one of the fathers of the Fauvist movement. "Darkened eyes, feeling the texture of the paint"[24] is what drew Galliano to van Dongen, and as a result his 2024 designs ride the knife's edge of grotesque feminine beauty.

Galliano's Look 28, on page 140, is a "boudoir-coloured tulle dress…worn over a stretch-tulle gloved bodysuit aquarelled in the grammar of Kees van Dongen, under-pinned by a boudoir-coloured silk satin cincher and a silicone hip prothèse matching the skin tone of the muse." Its "abstract-embroidery tulle mask" is painted with watercolor techniques in the Fauvist style meant to invoke a "dégradé of the senses."[25]

The looks were achieved with a variety of body modifiers such as corsets and prostheses that exaggerated breasts, hips, and butts, making it seem that the body was

Kees Van Dongen, *Femme au Grand Chapeau*, 1906

that of the model. In the collection's film, *Nighthawk*, Galliano describes the look as "a body that you wore." He wanted the viewer to be fooled into thinking the dress was painted right on their skin and used merkins (pubic wigs) to help in the artifice. The merkin, he says, added to women's feminine power, giving them a sense of liberation and control.

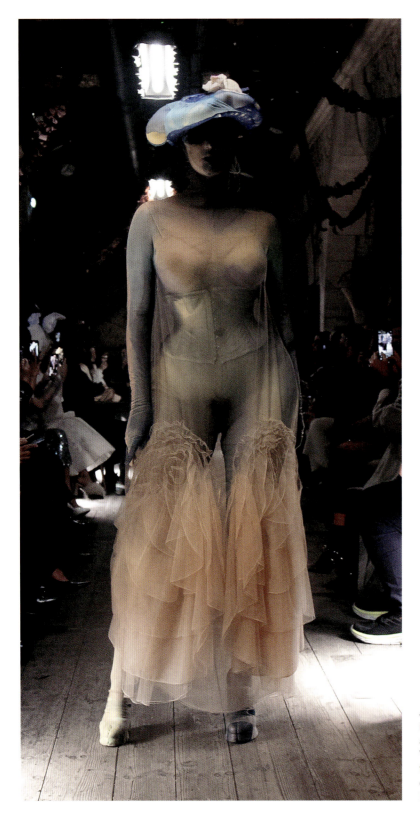

John Galliano was inspired by the decay and mystery of Kees Van Dongen's paintings for his S/S 2024 Couture collection for Maison Martin Margiela.

BENDING THE RULES: FASHION BEYOND THE BINARY

SPORTSMANLIKE CONDUCT

The sound of American football announcers and marching bands filters in and out of Baroque classical music as Thom Browne's Spring 2020 menswear collection parades by at the École des Beaux-Arts on a hot day. The heat is appropriate considering the setting's garden party theme, which includes trompe l'oeil topiaries and danseurs in pancake tutus dancing en pointe. Browne's pastel seersucker collection is a whimsical masculine fantasy featuring paniers to widen the hips and codpieces worn over wide skirts, pants, and overcoats. The look includes brogue heels with sports soles and mismatched athletic socks, boy's uniform jackets and striped ties, and cockades arranged organically like flowers. Models carry with them canopy-less parasols and leather bags resembling dachshunds, soccer balls, footballs, and basketballs.

Fashion commentator Bliss Foster writes that Browne plays with "uniformity and how it renders you anonymous, surrealism, and kind of a vague sense of the Kafkaesque, but also humor…a way of keeping things light and pleasant."[26] While his designs are rooted in rugged sports and the conformity of the corporate world, he challenges the idea that these masculine

Thom Browne's Menswear S/S 2020 show in Paris was described as "A Bunch of Ball Bags, Basically," by YouTuber Bliss Foster.

institutions must be sober and flavorless. Instead, he uses sportsmanship and the notion of the uniform to encourage self-expression, liberation, and imagination.

NICOLE HOUFF
BOUDOIR BARBIE

No exploration of feminine power would be complete without a glance at Barbie, an icon of both liberation and fetishization. But after the boudoir door is closed, the day is done, and the gaze of the public is gone, what does Barbie do after hours? This, and other questions, are answered by photographer Nicole Houff as she creates hyperrealistic scenarios where Barbie (and sometimes Ken) expand their universe beyond the Dreamhouse.

I interviewed Houff to learn how she creates her work and why she thinks Barbie is a powerful role model.

Benda: When choosing Barbie's clothes for your photographs, in what ways do you consider gender and femininity?

Houff: Admittedly, when I think about the clothes for the shoots, my choices are dictated by the scene itself and what doll I'm using. What I do consider probably more than anything is color and how it plays into the scene. For example, for *After Hours Barbie* [shown here], I knew that I wanted the entire photo to be a soft pink, which has instinctual associations (granted, totally man-made associations) with femininity, which I play into. In other words, I very purposely used all pink for her outfit, but the counterbalance is that I strive to elevate Barbie to a position of power, not a passive subject to be gazed at.

Benda: After the recent *Barbie* movie and all the discussion about feminism and women's roles in society, has your perception of Barbie's gender presentation changed?

Houff: I don't think my perception has changed, as I've been using her as the strong, dominant protagonist in my photos all along. What I think has changed is that other people are viewing her as a more powerful role model. The movie revitalized these larger societal discussions concerning femininity, what that looks like, that it's not mutually exclusive to feminism, and how that relates to a doll that was introduced in 1959. Honestly, I feel like the movie helped to elevate Barbie's gender presentation to be more multifaceted.

Benda: What inspired you to start creating the scenarios?

Houff: I'm often asked: Why Barbie? I never have a succinct answer for this. I feel like I started using Barbie in my art because of a perfect alignment of various factors. Of course, I love Barbie. And I've always wanted to be an artist. And I'm drawn to 1950s and 1960s aesthetics in art, design, advertising, pop culture—you name it. Barbie is the catalyst for me to create and explore these vignettes in the studio that speak to my visual interests and my sense of humor.

Nicole Houff's work, like this *After Hours* Barbie photograph, is meticulous and technical, down to tiny costume details, accessories, and props.

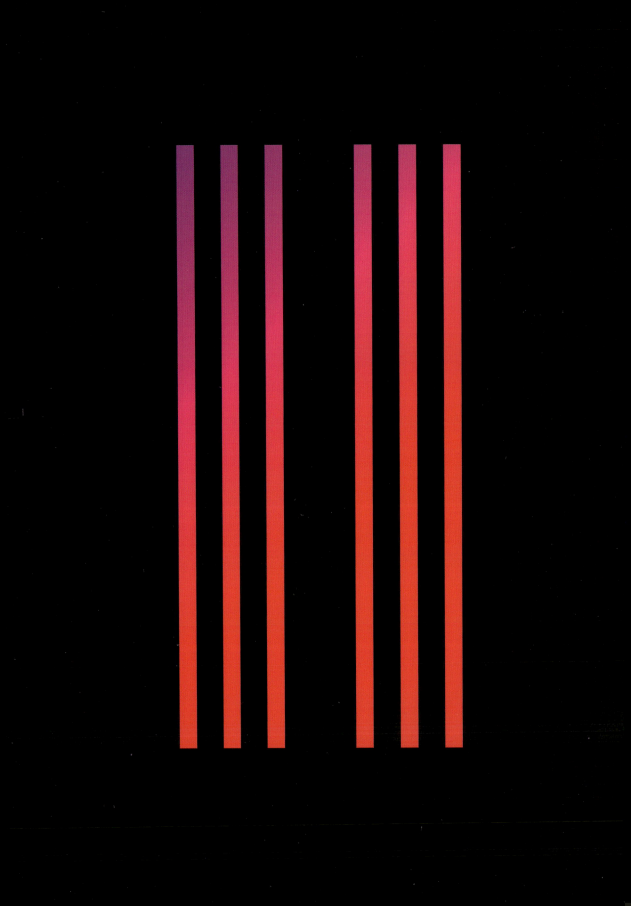

(DUALITY)

What happens when we look at the mirror image of ourselves? Our bodies can carry infinite versions of who we are, but this chapter looks specifically at how we can hold two opposing gender expressions in one physical body: masculine and feminine, split in two, visually defined by what we wear, allowed to play both roles or to just play! If we don't have to choose, we can freely switch between a traditionally masculine, dark, two-piece business suit and a sparkly sequined babydoll dress like artist Grayson Perry does. Or as actor Michael Urie did for the Met Gala, shown opposite, we can wear both sides of ourselves at one time.

Traditionally masculine with the inherent duality of black-and-white fabrics, tuxedos are the perfect tool for honoring our double selves. Black lesbian Harlem-based club impresario Gladys Bentley wore an all-white tailcoat ensemble, nonbinary actor Emma Corrin donned a reimagined cream tuxedo with black accessories in homage to an iconic outfit worn by Princess Diana, and actor Billy Porter perfected the gender-bending tuxedo ball gown for public appearances. It's no surprise that many of the individuals featured in this chapter are performers, athletes, or entertainers. They get to satisfy both sides of their identity by creating alter egos, allowing their bodies to be containers for gender experimentation and their fashion to be nonverbal, visual representations.

It's not just modern individuals who get to have all the fun, though. Eighteenth-century fencing masters, nineteenth-century dandies and writers, and ancient Egyptian, Elizabethan, and seventeenth-century female rulers explored how fashion and dress could represent the complex identities they built to navigate a male-dominated world.

Historically, women's duality focused on gaining power through men's clothing, while men's duality was nostalgic for an innocent childhood. While women used menswear as a uniform of authority, men already had that authority and so could dress like little boys while still hanging on to the power that automatically came with their birth gender. As Grayson Perry observes in his 2016 book *The Descent of Man*, "Gender may be a performance, but it is not playing pretend."[1] Fashion helps us perform our gender but shouldn't be taken lightly—underneath the clothes can be authentic representations of ourselves. Duality is black and white, light and dark, masculine and feminine, soft and hard, chiffon and leather.

OPPOSITE
Michael Urie poses on the red carpet at the Metropolitan Museum of Art Costume Institute Benefit Gala in 2019.

THE DUALITY OF BLACK AND WHITE

In need of an informal dinner look, fashion rebel Prince Edward asked Savile Row tailors Henry Poole & Sons to make him a brand-new style of jacket in 1865. Poole & Sons made a tailored jacket in "celestial blue" wool cloth with a silk satin shawl collar, one button, and, most notably, no tails. Edward would have recognized the informal heritage of a shawl collar: eighteenth-century smoking jackets and robes worn only at home were tailored with a silk shawl collar.

American socialites took note of the new evening coat style worn by Edward, brought it to New York's Tuxedo Park Club on Tuxedo Lake, and the name became history. Tailcoats, tuxedos, smoking jackets, and dinner jackets existed concurrently, but the tuxedo has become shorthand for formal dress. Variations were limitless as the tuxedo evolved from exclusively shawl-collared versions to a wide range of lapels and colors expanded past black and celestial blue. Now a deconstructed tuxedo might only keep a few of the original details, but everyone still knows the reference.

Harlem nightclub owner and lesbian icon Gladys Bentley poses in a white top hat and tails.

RIGHT
A 1901 fashion plate depicting men's formal dress.

BELOW
Fred Astaire's white tie headshot for the film *You'll Never Get Rich* from 1941.

BOTTOM
Legendary gay artist J. C. Leyendecker became famous for creating Arrow Collars & Shirts advertising that clandestinely catered to the gay male gaze, like this tableau of men in formalwear punctuated by one woman in a coral pink evening dress.

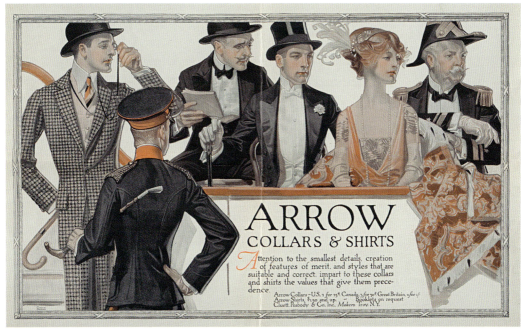

ARROW
COLLARS & SHIRTS

*A*ttention to the smallest details, creation of features of merit, and styles that are suitable and correct, impart to these collars and shirts the values that give them precedence.

Arrow Collars – U.S. 2 for 25¢. Canada, 3 for 50¢ Great Britain, 2 for 1/- Arrow Shirts, $1.50 and up. Booklets on request Cluett, Peabody & Co. Inc. Makers Troy, N.Y.

OPPOSITE
Legendary performer Joséphine Baker gender-bends in men's formalwear, 1930.

ABOVE
1920's double act Les Rocky Twins match their looks, hair, and makeup.

DUALITY

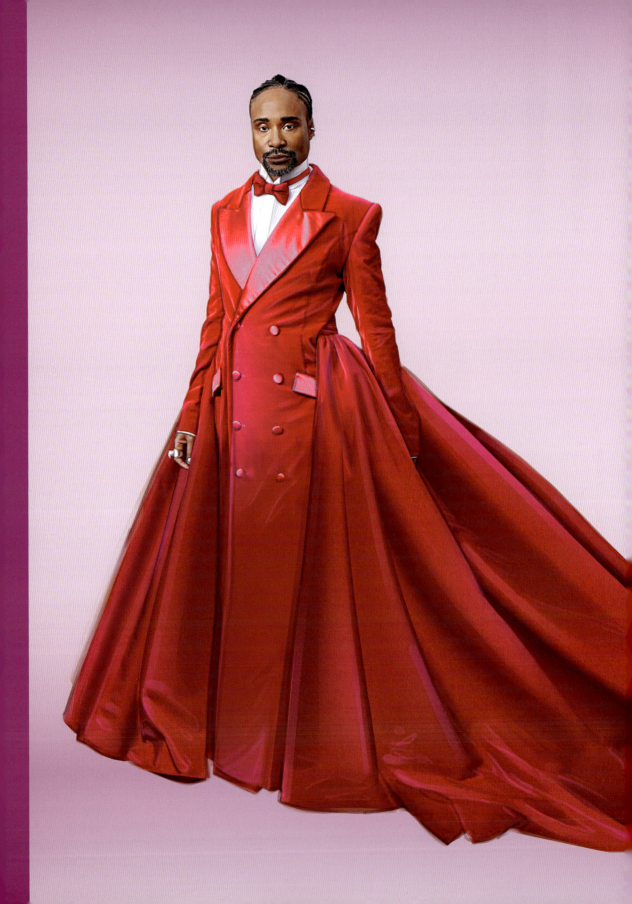

BILLY PORTER: THE TUXEDO BALL GOWN

An excited murmur followed actor Billy Porter from the plush red carpet to the steps of the Met Gala. Though he'd previously worn brilliant ensembles, Porter sparked the conversation around men's splendor in 2019 when he wore a tuxedo gown by red-carpet stalwart Christian Siriano to the Oscars. The black velvet masterpiece, with its classic satin pique lapels and velvet bow tie, instantly stole the show, but instead of tuxedo trousers, it featured a nipped waist and voluminous skirt. Siriano's ensemble balanced the masculine ideals of subdued refinement with a confident stroke of opulence that inspired a cascade of cross-gender formalwear.

Siriano also designed the tuxedo gown illustrated here: a magenta satin and silk velvet ensemble Porter wore to the Golden Globes in 2023.

Gowns became Porter's calling card, and his showstopping elegance opened the red carpet to other men interested in experimenting with beauty. Porter described his creative process in 2020: "When you're an actor, the clothes are part of the character, the clothes help create what the character becomes."[2] His perspective on gender identity connects with fashion as well:

> I think the world is ready for a different conversation surrounding gender and what we can and cannot wear. You know, it's like men have been wearing dresses, if we're going to call it that, since the beginning of time, you go back to the Greeks. Jesus wore a robe! They were in robes, we call them robes, but it's the same thing—it's a dress. So what's the problem? Why is it a problem?[3]

DECONSTRUCTED TUXES

Although Billy Porter is a tough act to follow, Lalisa Manobal from the K-pop band Blackpink holds her own. Wearing a Markgong tuxedo dress and floor-length white shirt with black trousers, Manobal blends feminine and masculine trends for maximum impact. Manobal joins generations of women adopting and subverting tuxedos throughout the twentieth century. After WWI, when smoky interwar Berlin night-clubs briefly allowed freedom of dress before the maelstrom of WWII began, tuxedos were a way for women to queer men's fashion. Marlene Dietrich famously cross-dressed in tailcoat and top hat in the 1930 film *Morocco*. In 1960s London, youth-quake ingenues with pixie cuts took on men's formal dress, and in 1966 Paris, Yves Saint Laurent debuted his ultra-sleek and sexy "Le Smoking" women's tuxedo.

Similarly, Emma Corrin is crafting a nonbinary red-carpet image in this Miu Miu tuxedo ensemble, sans trousers. Corrin and their stylist, Harry Lambert, are now well known for concocting cutting-edge red-carpet looks for premieres and award shows. At a 2023 party for the television series *The Crown*, Corrin paired the cream silk tuxedo jacket with black leather gloves, a sheer cream floor-length column skirt, a black bow tie, knee-high black socks, and chunky Mary Jane platforms. Sheer fabric often signifies a transitional fashion moment; in this case, it not only telegraphs the "pants-less" red-carpet trend but also adds a twist to long-skirt formality. The tuxedo has become a symbol of formality, free of ball gowns and evening dresses, across the gender spectrum.

OPPOSITE
Lalisa Manobal twists the tuxedo on the Oscars awards ceremony red carpet, 2025.

RIGHT
Emma Corrin arriving at the London finale celebration for *The Crown*, season 6, in 2023.

THE CHEVALIER D'ÉON AND MADEMOISELLE CHARLOTTE

By the time the young military officer Monsieur Beaumont left the house in eighteenth-century Paris to step into a carriage, they would have spent hours on adornment, fashion, grooming, and makeup. Dressing in the eighteenth century was a complicated, expensive, and time-consuming business, and the more powerful and wealthy you were, the more complicated your clothes were. Typically, aristocratic dress was purposely restrictive and impractical—it showed that you didn't have to do manual labor. The servants that maintained your home and furniture, cooked for you, and carried your letters would also dress you and preserve your fine garments.

Born in 1728 as Charles, Chevalier d'Éon de Beaumont (a dizzying array of future names and pronouns awaited) to a noble family of modest means, they would have spent their first five years of life in France being dressed by servants in typical children's wear: dresses. Both boys and girls wore the same garments, along with long hair, stockings, and soft shoes. At around eight years old, the young Monsieur Beaumont's servants would begin dressing them in a miniature version of adult menswear: a three-piece suit of a coat, waistcoat, and breeches, complete with chemise, stockings, and leather shoes. Later, ritualistic and regimented military menswear would be the chevalier's gender signal as they moved up the ranks of the French military as a soldier, spy, and diplomat (the French order of *Chevalier* is given as a knightly honor) and eventually deployed to London at King Louis XV's request.

After forty-nine years dressing as a man, Monsieur Beaumont became Mademoiselle Charlotte (despite the loss of power and status that their male gender presentation would have automatically conferred). Around 1771 rumors began circulating that the chevalier was dressing (and competitively fencing) as a woman, wearing a complex set of petticoats, chemises, corsets, bum rolls, hip padding, bodices, skirts, mobcaps, jewelry, stockings, silk satin shoes, kidskin gloves, and perhaps a cape or caraco. By 1777, Mademoiselle Charlotte was fully living as a woman, meaning they were one of the few well-known eighteenth-century individuals who intimately knew what it felt like to wear women's and men's dress plus military uniform. The chevalier wore eighteenth-century ladies' heels as easily as heavy leather service boots.

In the digital illustration on page 156, based on paintings and engravings of Mademoiselle Charlotte, they wear a closed-front robe à l'anglaise with a lace-edged fichu, a powdered wig in the late-Baroque le pouf hairstyle, the St. George's Cross (which had never before been worn upon women's clothing), and leather camel fencing gloves. Their two ostrich feathers are a symbol of patriotism, while their loosely arranged silk ribbon cockade is more a fashion statement than a political badge.

In the tumult of the French Revolution, the chevalier lost their pension around 1789,

fenced for money to scrape by, and died penniless in 1810. A hand-painted color autopsy drawing by Charles Turner in the collection of the British Museum notes the chevalier's birth gender: "I hereby certify that I have inspected & dissected the Body of the Chevalier d'Éon, in the presence of Mr. Adair, Mr. Wilson, & Le père Elisée, & have found the Male Organs in every respect, perfectly formed."[4] Yet contemporary engravings and caricatures, like those featured here, showed the chevalier as a split, dual being: one side dressed in men's clothes, the other in women's.

BENDING THE RULES: FASHION BEYOND THE BINARY

Hail! Thou Production most uncommon,
Woman half-man and man half-Woman!

Vid: Epistle.

CHARLES PIERCE
DOUBLE EXPOSURE

Switching from ladies' heels to men's leather lace-up shoes was part of daily life for actor and entertainer Charles Pierce. When Pierce started his performing career in 1954, a tuxedo was the costume of choice for his first appearance at Los Angeles's Club La Vie. He went on stage in what was then considered women's wear, becoming a cult favorite, a club fixture, and a TV guest star who transfixed audiences with his interpretations of famous actresses.

In LA, while some gay and lesbian venues like Club La Vie were open to the public, an underground network of private homes also hosted gatherings where LGBTQ+ individuals could dress as they wished, not as society wanted them to. Homemade posters and flyers, mimeographed onto colored sheets of paper, advertised the address of the house. Guests were encouraged to arrive quietly wearing street clothes and, once inside, to change into whatever truly reflected their identity: drag, jeans and a tee, bondage, leather, or fancy dress.

This original 1970s photograph, double exposed, shows the duality of Pierce's career. On one side is Pierce in men's formal wear; on the other, Pierce in female drag, his arms overlapping in the middle.

BENDING THE RULES: FASHION BEYOND THE BINARY

THE MASQUERADE LAW

They weren't masked, they weren't in disguise, they weren't farmers, and they weren't armed. Nevertheless, police officers arrested a group of forty-four male drag ball attendees on an October 1962 evening in Manhattan. The reasoning? An obscure 1845 New York State anti-masquerade law meant to stop rebellious male farmers from disguising themselves as Indigenous women in calico dresses to avoid paying land rent.

The twentieth-century interpretation of this informal "Three Article Rule" was that any citizen wearing fewer than three articles of clothing (except socks!) from their birth gender could be arrested for cross-dressing. Of course, cross-dressers found ingenious ways to outwit the police, hiding gendered pieces of clothing under their outfits and shopping at unisex boutiques.

Original text of the "masquerade law" used to prosecute cross-dressers, New York Consolidated Laws, Penal Law Article 240.35(4), Loitering, passed January 28, 1845, repealed June 13, 2020: "Being masked or in any manner disguised by unusual or unnatural attire or facial alteration, loiters, remains or congregates in a public place with other persons so masked or disguised, or knowingly permits or aids persons so masked or disguised to congregate in a public place; except that such conduct is not unlawful when it occurs in connection with a masquerade party or like entertainment if, when such entertainment is held in a city which has promulgated regulations in connection with such affairs, permission is first obtained from the police or other appropriate authorities."[5]

HE'S ALL YOURS

A drag queen is arrested by the
New York Police Department
in 1962.

"New York City resident Martin Boyce recalls that on Halloween,
1968, a cop collared him in Queens because his Oscar Wilde
costume was too feminine. Boyce argued back, brandishing the
receipts from the unisex store where he'd bought his clothes.
Their argument attracted the attention of a nearby gang. The police
officer, frustrated by Boyce's resistance, acquiesced to Boyce's
arguments—and then turned to the gang, saying, 'He's all yours.'
The gang was so amused by Boyce's defiant attitude,
they let him pass unharmed."[6]

GENDER RIGID

Sometimes he's the Turner Prize–winning ceramicist Grayson Perry, sometimes he's a cheerful, exuberant, outgoing cross-dresser called Claire. This duality of spirit flows throughout Perry's creative practice as an artist, permeates his daily life, and challenges what it means to be a modern man. Alan Measles, Perry's childhood teddy bear, pops up throughout his work as a symbol of masculinity but also exudes the innocence of a child's toy.

Perry engages the public about gender identity (and fashion) on multiple levels, as an artist, broadcaster (*Grayson's Art Club, Grayson Perry: All Man*), and writer (*The Descent of Man, Portrait of the Artist as a Little Girl*). The two portraits on pages 164 and 165 by award-winning photographer Pål Hansen show Grayson in his daily masculine dress and as his alter ego, Claire. Grayson's everyday dress—T-shirts, sneakers, and jeans—are the urban uniform of millions of men, and Claire's feminine, colorful, sequined dress carries an element of the masculine as well: a sequined men's necktie is appliqued to the torso. Hansen blogged about his process collaborating with Perry on these images:

> This shoot with Grayson was looking at the issue of identity. The idea for the shoot was to capture Grayson on two different days with comparable poses. One day dressed as Claire and the other as Grayson. The issue with this is of course to try to get the light to be the exact same but mirrored. It was never to be 100% accurate but I like the small differences as well as it makes it slightly more genuine and reveals that the images are not just "flipped."[7]

"Here's what I am, I'm Grayson Perry, Turner Prize winner—that's my full name [laughs]. We've all got a multiplicity of identities—what's our headline of our identity? It changes all the time. Here I am, I'm a father, I'm a husband, I'm a TV presenter."[8]

"No one's as sexist as a transvestite. We like gender roles. I always describe myself as gender rigid, I signed up for a gender and I want them to be very clearly delineated, so I know I'm dressing up in the wrong clothes."[9]

"During my later years at school, I was the proud owner of a camouflage army-issue combat jacket, which I teamed with a skinhead haircut. I think I adopted this very masculine uniform as a counterpoint to my rebellious sexuality that wanted flowery frills, heels, and makeup."[10]

OPPOSITE
Claire, Grayson Perry's alter ego, photographed by Pål Hansen, 2019.

LEFT
Grayson Perry photographed by Pål Hansen, 2019.

COMMANDO CHIC
NINETEENTH-CENTURY MALE VIRILITY

Beau Brummell and other Eton boys lined the flower-strewn streets of 1790s Windsor, England, demanding a toll from townspeople coming to town during Montem, a holiday of fancy-dress rebellion. The toll was to support the festival of springtime, fertility, and children that even in Brummell's time was considered ancient, dating back to the Middle Ages. The party had militaristic undertones, filled with revelry, drinking, seducing, and boyishly sadistic traditions. Young Brummell attended wearing the "poleman uniform," a mainstay of Eton schoolboys of a common or junior status. Biographer Ian Kelly writes:

> Indeed, this was the look of most of the school at Montem: a dark blue jacket with two rows of brass buttons, allowing a view of a white stock at the neck and paired with paler breeches. In contrast, the older boys dressed in a parody of courtiers and looked, deliberately, overdressed and ridiculous.[11]

Eton was an extremely masculine world where boys learned to dominate their social circles through mental, emotional, and physical power struggles. Nearly all the students experienced ritualistic violence and hazing, but Brummell consistently remained a jester: charming, charismatic, and witty. Uniforms became his sartorial armor, providing comfort and protection. Before finishing his education, he joined the tremendously fashionable Tenth Regiment of Light Dragoons, whose uniform closely reflected a more extravagant poleman. Ian Kelly describes the outfit:

> Dark blue, with pale yellow facings and silver-thread braiding.... There was a blue, sleeveless "upper jacket" or "shell" with braided epaulettes, cut long on the body and worn over a sleeved under-jacket. Both items were "frogged and looped" or embroidered with horizontal braiding in white satin and were further decorated with real silver tassels and "Elliot" balls.[12]

But to the lusty onlooker, the most astounding part of the uniform were the riding breeches. Kelly writes that they were "white, tight, trouser length and worn uncomfortably, considering they were a cavalry regiment, without underwear.... The marble-colored wool, woven on stocking looms, gave the rider's legs the appearance of nakedness."[13] When compared to the sexual dynamics of life at Eton, the buff uniform trousers become a highly erotic symbol of adolescence.

This duality of adolescent beauty and manly authority is a pattern across time. Nearly a century after Brummell's Montem festivities, poet Oscar Wilde became a sensation within the Aesthetic movement

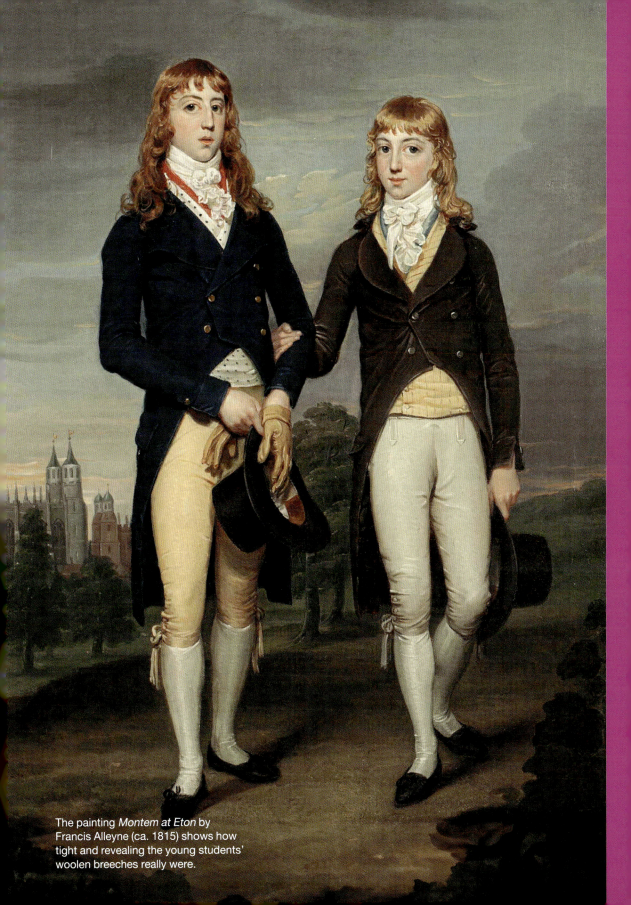

The painting *Montem at Eton* by Francis Alleyne (ca. 1815) shows how tight and revealing the young students' woolen breeches really were.

soldier and pioneer was the ideal of male identity. Wilde was an object of curiosity during his tour. American newspapers described him in both masculine and feminine terms: long limbed, taller, and more imposing than they expected, but with delicate features that women would envy. According to biographer Richard Ellman, Wilde

emerged to greet them clad in a great green coat that hung down almost to his feet. It was subjected to close inspection: the collar and cuffs were trimmed with seal or otter, and so was the material for the round cap, variously described as a smoking cap or a turban. Beneath the coat could be discerned a shirt with a wide Lord Byron collar and a sky-blue necktie, vaguely reminiscent of the costume of a modern mariner. He wore patent-leather shoes on his small feet.[15]

during his 1882 literary tour to America. Like Brummell, Wilde was inspired by school uniforms and social propriety. The pressure of trying to live openly as a gay man in a judgmental world was extreme, and he was jailed for his sexual orientation toward the end of his life. He expressed his preference for beautiful and ordered simplicity in his critique of fashion, "The Philosophy of Dress," in 1885: "I hold that dress is made for the service of Humanity. They think that Beauty is a matter of frills and furbelows. I care nothing at all for frills."[14]

Wilde was under constant physical scrutiny, especially in America, where the aggressive masculinity of the revolutionary

Possibly influenced by Wilde's lecture tour, Frances Hodgson Burnett dressed her son Vivian in clothes reflecting ideals of boyish beauty. She went on to write the children's serial *Little Lord Fauntleroy*. In the story, Cedric Errol, the cleverest and most gentlemanly little boy, fresh off the trauma of losing his father and sinking into poverty, cut "a graceful, childish figure in a black velvet suit, with a lace collar, and with lovelocks waving about the handsome, manly little face."[16] During the Victorian times the Fauntleroy suit was worn by boys until their tenth birthday, before they started their journey into manhood.

BENDING THE RULES: FASHION BEYOND THE BINARY

ABOVE

A boy's silk velvet Little Lord Fauntleroy suit complete with cap and ruffled cotton shirt from 1885.

TOP RIGHT

Little Lord Fauntleroy theatrical poster titled "I'm very glad I'm going to be an earl" from 1888.

RIGHT

Oscar Wilde in a boating-style schoolboy look, as photographed by longtime friend and collaborator Napoleon Sarony in New York City in 1883.

美少年
BEAUTIFUL BOYS

Björn Johan Andrésen, a Swedish actor known for playing the fourteen-year-old Tadzio in Luchino Visconti's 1971 film adaptation of the Thomas Mann novella *Death in Venice*.

Beau Brummell and Oscar Wilde might seem far removed from 1970s Tokyo, but Brummell's rowdy adolescence and Wilde's aestheticism heavily inspired the godmother of manga sex, Keiko Takemiya, whose *The Poem of Wind and Trees* popularized the boys' love (BL) manga scene in Japan. Protagonist Gilbert Cocteau is a high-born beauty who leaves the reader wondering whether he's a boy or a man, just like the young man illustrated here. The bishōnen, or "beautiful boys," inspired by Takemiya's work, expressed their aesthetic beauty through collegiate and sailor styles and emulated the erotic softness of boyhood seen in characters such as Tadzio from Thomas Mann's *Death in Venice*. These manga artists purposefully blended the lines of childhood and adult content. This concept of childhood sexuality was powerful and liberating to the women who pioneered the boy love genre in Japan, as it gave both boys and women a sense of personal agency in a highly patriarchal society.

The bishōnen are the successor of the Edo period's wakashū, a transitional male third gender that was banned from public life at the start of the Meiji period. While wakashū expressed themselves through a blending of traditional Japanese men's and women's fashions, the bishonen blended Western conventions instead. Scholar Gregory M. Pflugfelder writes about the bishonen style:

> In some cases, the "beautiful boy" (bishōnen) of the Meiji imagination wore the contemporary guise of a student, other authors and artists pictured him as a sprightly naval cadet. Both icons of young male eroticism sported an identifying uniform.[17]

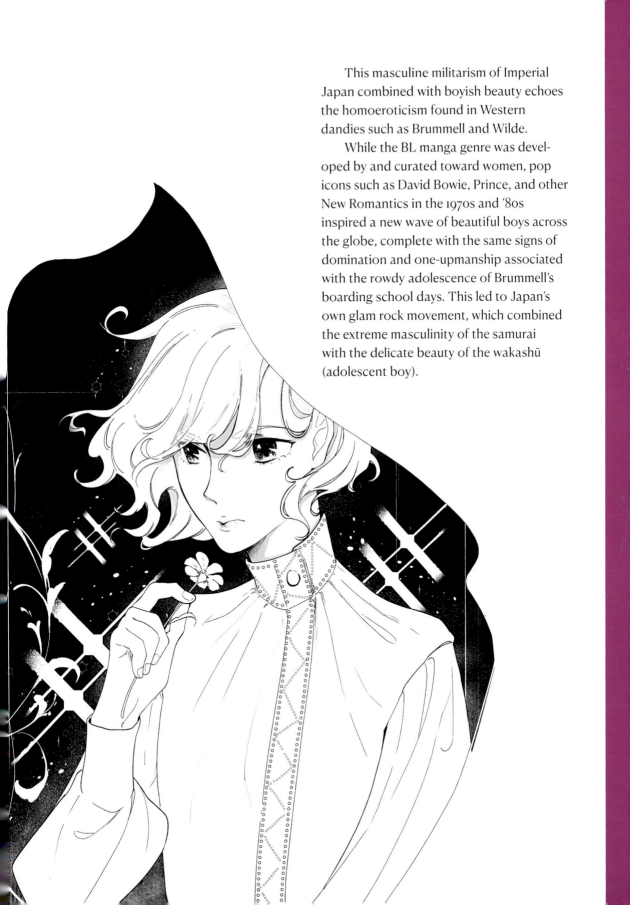

This masculine militarism of Imperial Japan combined with boyish beauty echoes the homoeroticism found in Western dandies such as Brummell and Wilde.

While the BL manga genre was developed by and curated toward women, pop icons such as David Bowie, Prince, and other New Romantics in the 1970s and '80s inspired a new wave of beautiful boys across the globe, complete with the same signs of domination and one-upmanship associated with the rowdy adolescence of Brummell's boarding school days. This led to Japan's own glam rock movement, which combined the extreme masculinity of the samurai with the delicate beauty of the wakashū (adolescent boy).

THE LOVE SYMBOL

"**A** purple sock was found inside each boot."[18] These purple socks are an ordinary human moment in the life of an extraordinary musical artist, Prince. A Smithsonian Institution curator wrote that short note about Prince's forgotten socks as they archived the famous footwear. Worn with a matching lavender suit of jacket and trousers, these lavender silk satin high-heeled boots weren't just a fashion statement. They were custom designed by Andre Rostomyan in Los Angeles to withstand performance after performance: heavy-duty dance rubber is glued onto the soles, and a metal shank heel support is essential to the design.

A pair of custom-made lavender heeled ankle boots worn by Prince for numerous occasions, with a matching ensemble, 1993–2000.

The gold metal pull tab on the boot zipper was Prince's Love Symbol. The artist designed it with Minneapolis branding specialist Mitch Monson to merge the female gender glyph (representing Venus) with the male gender glyph (representing Mars), adding a circular swirl to symbolize music. Prince changed his name to the Love Symbol on his thirty-fifth birthday in 1993, thus embodying his own duality. As he sang in "I Would Die 4 U," "I'm not a woman, I'm not a man / I am something that you'll never understand."[19] Prince's music contained gender-identity questions as well as answers. For "Controversy" he wrote, "Am I black or white? Am I straight or gay?"[20] As part of performing his unique gender identity, Prince created an alter ego, Camille. She was Prince's feminine side, inspired by nineteenth-century French intersex individual Alexina Barbin, who changed their name at twenty-two to Camille (a unisex name in France).

Perhaps these lilac silk ankle boots were just part of a costume, but with them Prince joined millions of high heel–wearing men throughout history. Seventeenth-century European cavalier shoes had stacked, two-inch heels, while 1970s platform boots added up to six inches of height to men wearing bell-bottoms and turtlenecks.

ESMAA MOHAMOUD
ONE OF THE BOYS

Describing her childhood dress code, Canadian artist Esmaa Mohamoud recalls that as a little girl wearing sports jerseys, "even at a young age I understood that I was a girl but I also wanted to perform my gender in a masculine way."[21] Like Prince, Mohamoud mixes masculine and feminine as a genuine self-expression in a binary world. As an internationally exhibited artist, she has created work like this 2017–2019 series *One of the Boys* (with Qendrim Hoti), which uses wide hoop skirts and jerseys from former basketball players (including Toronto Raptors' Vince Carter, shown here) to comment on professional sports and Black masculinity.[22]

Esmaa Mohamoud's 2017 artwork *One of the Boys [Red]* is crafted from silk, velvet, jersey, repurposed jersey, and shoelaces to create a striking sports jersey and ball gown hybrid garment.

"By invoking symbols of hyperfemininity (the ball gown) and hypermasculinity (the basketball jersey), Mohamoud and Hoti craft a space of gender fluidity that resists clear demarcation. With the models both adorned in gowns, displaying their backs to the cameras, there is a statement of defiance. These bodies refuse easy categorization."[23]

KYLE KUZMA

"SWAG IS SWAG. DRIP IS DRIP."

The sports star stereotype is a player who says everything they need to say on the court. Off the court, their words don't matter; Esmaa Mohamoud made art that spoke for them. Now, art is becoming reality, as basketball player Kyle Kuzma and fellow players speak with their fashion, but on a surprising liminal runway between home and court.

Kuzma wore a now-famous, truly gigantic, pink cable-knit sweater for one of his tunnel walks, where the short distance to the locker room from an athlete's car or the team bus has become a fashion runway. Kuzma and stylist Toreno Winn saw the Fall/Winter 2021 Raf Simons garment as a deliberate, personal, and authentic fashion choice. The press and fellow players saw it as a wild, provocative, viral moment.

Yet Kuzma is part of a new generation of athletes who are saying what's on their minds through their clothes. Photographers line up to capture players' swag, and social media amplifies luxury brands and in-the-know new designers. Male athletes like Kuzma are embracing their true style,

wearing bright colors, bold patterns, and experimental pieces that might not be classically masculine.

Female athletes like Angel Reese can also dress to be themselves, rather than conforming to a typically feminine stereotype, mixing tailored suiting with sequined gowns and bodycon minidresses. Since many professional players are world-renowned superstars, their endorsement of androgynous, playful, and gender-bending styles trickles down to regular fans. In a Winter 2025 *Vogue* article, journalist Maya Singer describes the stadium as a runway and notes that the tunnel walk "became a promenade of dandies the likes of which hadn't been seen since Beau Brummell strode the cobblestones of Mayfair."[24]

KING NJINGA

In the subtropical coastal kingdom of Ndongo (in modern Angola), Njinga Mbande was born into royalty in 1583, the daughter of King Mbande a Ngola. Instead of conforming to typical female roles of the time, the adult Njinga went in a radically different direction to secure the future of her kingdom, which was under attack from colonial forces. She remade herself into a female king, using both her gender and her spirituality as political tools to secure her power, choosing the most advantageous armor at any given time. Many of her contemporaries—including her adversaries, the Portuguese—questioned the wisdom of a woman ruler, but she didn't see her gender as being dictated by her body. By donning the behaviors, roles, and clothing of men, Njinga *became* a man. According to biographer Linda M. Heywood,

> She began her transition...by marrying a man, Ngola Ntombo, and she insisted that he dress as a woman. She referred to him as female while demanding that he address her as king instead of queen. At the time of her marriage, she increased the number of male concubines she kept and ordered them to dress in the same clothing as her female bodyguards.[25]

Keeping her power was another story, and Njinga, like other female leaders before her, was pragmatic. She used fashion to assimilate to European standards, even wearing Christian icons when trading with the Portuguese. Through trade, King Njinga had access to perfumes and adornments[26] and used those to mix African dress (like the Kuba cloth shown on page 178) and European dress to her advantage.

This illustration is based in part on a 2002 statue in Luanda, Angola. It's likely that her chest was covered because of Catholic sentiments about nudity, rather than historical fact.

IS NJINGA MBANDE WEARING A KUBA CLOTH?

A panel of traditionally woven raffia
Kuba cloth from the twentieth century.

The answer is: maybe.

Today Kuba cloth (named for the Kuba people) is famous for its
dazzling geometry, but this aesthetic didn't evolve until the nineteenth
century at the height of the Kingdom of Kongo's power. Njinga
Mbande's statue in Luanda, Angola, is suggestive of earlier traditional
Kuba patterns, particularly diamond and dots, dyed with local
iron-rich clays. Many of these expertly woven cloths were and are still
worn for prestige and power, but no Kuba cloth from her time
has survived, so we can only guess.[27]

AMAZON WARRIORS
AGOJIE

Father Francesco Borghero marveled one humid afternoon in 1861 in Dahomey's capital as the king's elite warriors performed a military exercise in the dusty stone streets. Dressed in brown blouses, blue and brown knee breeches, caps, and sashes to carry their weapons, the warriors were an infamous, ferocious sight.[28] They fought barefoot through bloody, thorny acacia branches and strapped thorny belts to their waists as trophies to prove their might.[29] These fierce warriors were known to the Europeans as Dahomey Amazons, but in their own language of Fon are called agojie.

They likely began as third-ranked wives of the king that were unfit to bear children and therefore took on a masculine warrior role that gave them more stability. Like King Nzinga, the agojie warriors shifted genders as their status in society changed. Rather than tying their gender to their bodies, their gender was tied to how they adorned it and what type of work and prestige their fashion signified.

"As the blacksmith takes an iron bar and by fire changes its fashion, so we have changed our nature. We are no longer women, we are men."[50]

PHARAOH HATSHEPSU(T)

In the Valley of the Kings, where the sun casts its golden rays as far as the eye can see, the Pharaoh Hatshepsut II built their final resting place at Djeser-Djeseru. At the entrances of their temple, colossal kneeling statues and sphinxes adorned in the pharaoh's striped blue and yellow nemes headcloth project stately, masculine power. But once you venture further into the halls of Djeser-Djeseru, into the more private upper terraces and chapels, depictions of them become more feminine and fluid.[31]

According to the Metropolitan Museum of Art, "The ideal king was a young man in the prime of life,"[32] which gave Hatshepsut patriarchal and divine pressure to assure their subjects that they were the rightful ruler of Egypt. Their public image transformed into that of the ideal pharaoh—a young man with wide shoulders dressed in the shendyt kilt and nemes headdress. They wore a golden beard, had their skin tone painted red like a man rather than yellow like a woman, and even dropped the feminine *t* at the end of their name. "The physical reality was of less importance, so an old man, a child, or even a woman who held the titles of pharaoh could be represented in this ideal form."[33]

As with Njinga Mbande, the truth of Hatshepsut's gender and the male clothing they chose to wear wasn't a matter of biology. Gender in ancient Egypt was critical to creation myths and therefore the role of the pharaoh on Earth. According to trans historian Kit Heyam, "Maleness and femaleness were complementary aspects of an essential duality" of the gods, which meant that Hatshepsut's gender was "inseparable from their social role: to be Pharaoh, in ancient Egyptian culture, was to be male."[34]

The balance of "maleness and femaleness" might have been a feature of Hatshepsut's identity. Their pronouns were mixed in historical texts and graffiti, by both common people and official records. For example, statues of Hatshepsut in the masculine shendyt kilt with wide shoulders and a flat chest were accompanied by feminine titles and pronouns.

Catharine Roehrig at the Metropolitan Museum of Art explains that "this rather schizophrenic projection of her gender has been interpreted as an assertion of androgyny, a characteristic of fertility gods and creator gods."[35] Hapi and Wadj-Wer were both fertility gods with male pronouns, breasts, and the ability to become pregnant, for example. "But it was also a way of ensuring [sic] that both kingly identity and feminine gender were attached to the images, allowing them to function as intermediaries with the gods." In other words, Hatshepsut embodied both sides of divine duality.

Hatshepsut continued the practice of combining divine genders through their daughter, Princess Neferure. According to reliefs in Deir el-Bahari, Neferure wore

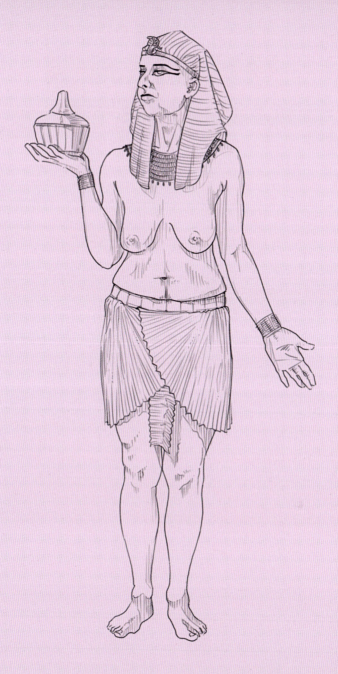

diadems and girdles, "one of the few jewelry forms worn exclusively by women," but was also carved sitting on her tutor Senenmut's lap while wearing a masculine false beard.

ABOVE
For this digital pencil drawing, Gwyn Conaway referenced the writings of journalist Katarina Kratovac to recreate Hatshepsut in their late forties, when

their public image and lived reality differed greatly. Based on the *Seated Statue of Hatshepsut* at the Metropolitan Museum of Art, Hatshepsut wears the pharaoh's nemes headcloth and men's pleated shendyt kilt, and eye kohl makeup. Their matronly figure is informed by mummy KV60A, identified by Egyptologist Dr. Zahi Hawass as that of Hatshepsut. There are no surviving details regarding ornament at their waist, so the belt is nondescript. They hold a nemset vessel that was found in their tomb.

QUEEN ELIZABETH I

For Queen Elizabeth I, being a woman was a double-edged sword. She sat on a precarious pedestal in patriarchal England, and, because her culture saw gender and sex as the same thing, she had to play a delicate balancing game for the entirety of her seventy-year reign. She managed her image by wielding dual weapons: the ferocity of a Tudor king (her father was Henry VIII) and the divinity of a virgin.

Elizabeth I didn't exactly disguise herself as a man, but she did adopt doublets fashioned in a men's silhouette, with round chests and nipped waistlines, as seen in this photograph. In the 1575 *Darnley Portrait*, she combined men's tailoring with opulent skirts and women's cosmetics. In the 1601 *Rainbow Portrait*, she wore a golden cape embroidered with eyes and ears. She wanted her subjects to know that she could both hear and see them no matter where her gaze was focused, and, despite their protests, remind them that her power was absolute.

Unlike King Nzinga Mbande or Hatshepsut, Elizabeth I embraced images of maidenhood in service to the kingdom and started wearing black and white as a symbol of her chastity. Elizabeth's brand of virginity was a striking, virile, and unrelenting image.

A men's Jerkin from western Europe around 1580, made from leather, silk, linen, cotton, and similar in shape to the styles that Elizabeth I wore.

She combined the red curls and pale skin that marked her as an ageless beauty with masculine military touches like gold braid, tassels, and buttons, as in the portrait opposite. She demanded fear and love in equal measure, playing both sides of the binary coin. "Let tyrants fear," she said to her troops at Tilbury in 1588. "I know I have the body of a weak and feeble woman; but I have the heart and stomach of a king."[36]

"When Elizabeth is in her private apartments, she can have her wig off, she can wear a shift, she can be an ageing woman. That's the private Elizabeth: she is a human being with a body that will deteriorate. As soon as she walks out of the doors of her private apartment, she is the Queen, and she must look like the Queen. She is on parade and her dress is vital."[37]

(TRIAD)

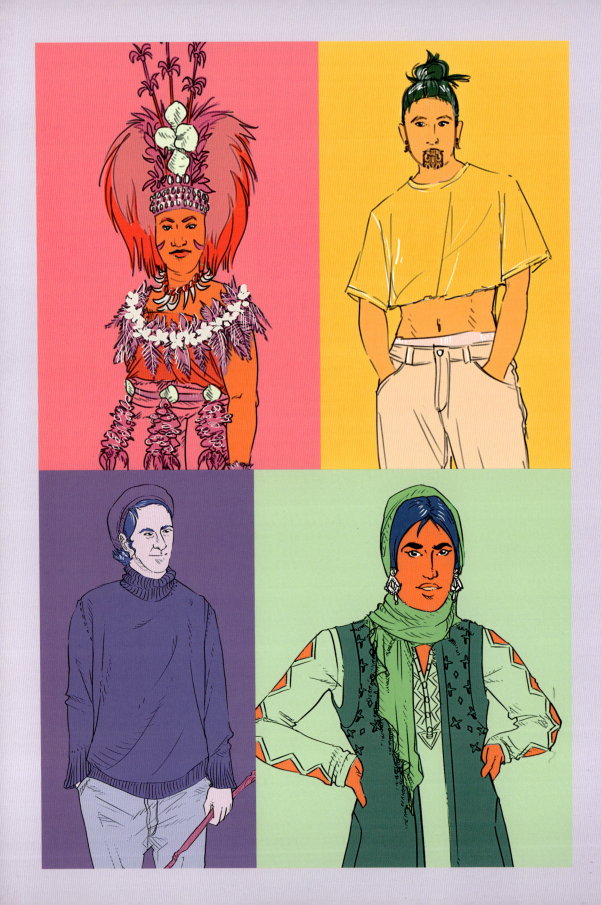

What happens when society leaves space for gender identities that expand beyond male and female to spiritual, shamanistic, and ceremonial roles? The trailblazing individuals in this section are the answer. Their experience is universal; we all have a gender identity, so we can all relate to their stories. When sharing this rich history, author Kit Heyam looked to our collective ancestors: "Their stories still show that there is a long, cross-cultural history of understanding gender as not binary, not fixed, and not tied to the body."[1]

Language reflects culture. The English language isn't equipped to honor all the cultural roles that third-gender, Two-Spirit, and nonbinary individuals have occupied in society across time and around the globe. But many languages are, so global words for nonbinary and gender-nonconforming people are thousands of years old. Some of the many examples include łachmana, bòte, kannith, hijra, mukannath, muxes, fa'afafine, fa'afatama, māhū, takatapui, wakashū, kathoey, samyaan, winkte, burrneshë, tainna, wa'ippe, hwame, aqi, calalai, and babaylan.

Fashion, traditional dress, and personal style outside the binary have existed for millennia, as have genderfluid individuals. As Heyam writes, "When we put on something that changes the way we feel about our gender…we share that experience with thousands of people from the past."[2] It's thrilling to see the infinite ways we combine fashion and dress to innovatively communicate our identities. Beginning with the drag king performances of London-based artist Whiskey Chow, moving to Dan Taulapapa McMullin's full-body flower suit, and concluding with historical reimaginings of Congolese and Brazilian jinbandaa shamans, the past comes to life, meeting a dynamic present and visioning a vibrant future.

CLOCKWISE FROM TOP LEFT
Fa'afatama (Samoan culture); Takatāpui (Māori culture); Mukhannath (Arabic culture); Sworn Virgin (Albania)

"To restrict ourselves to static, binary gender is to fall short of our potential—both as human beings, and as whatever else we might have the capacity to be."[3]

WHISKEY CHOW
BARE HAND, EMPTY FIST

As a self-described "artivist," Whiskey Chow explodes boundaries, approaching their experimental work in performance, moving images, sound, installation, and printmaking with the mind of an activist. Sausages, molded plastic, body paint, tape, mushrooms, passport photographs, balloons, electric blenders, stick-on mustaches, corn syrup, blow-up dolls, Chinese spices, blue powder, and black licorice are just some of the materials that Chow uses to create visceral, immersive, and interdisciplinary performances. For them, being an artivist means making art with a heart of activism.

In 2016, Chow began creating a new way of performing drag. They referenced traditional Chinese male opera characters, including their full-face makeup, to produce a queer reading of the cultural practice. Chow has also generated the avatar Phoenix Chow to tell stories of Chinese mythology and gender identity. Also known as Whiskey's digital queer hero (queero), Phoenix is based on martial arts superstar Bruce Lee. Here, Chow talks about the stainless-steel sculpture of Phoenix Chow shown opposite and a recurring theme in their work, the masculine torso.

Benda: In your work with Phoenix Chow, and other figures like Stretch Armstrong, how do you approach the masculine torso?

Chow: I do think toys are like sculptures, and for me they can be an entry point to open space for vulnerability and some kind of emotional space to explore different kinds of masculinity. The silicone torso shape is very charged with toughness and hypermasculinity. When I put on a silicone torso on stage, it creates a softness. Each torso for me is different; they show different possibilities to negotiate with masculinity.

As a child, I went to school with a lot of boys' toys in my little bag. And then every morning, I carried the bag to the kindergarten, and I knew I would be a star when I opened my bag. I loved that all the boys would come—I got to choose who I would like to play with. In kindergarten I didn't want to wear a girl's dress. I always wore my own T-shirt and short pants from a very early age to demonstrate my position or to visualize my way with masculinity.

Benda: The collared white shirt and waistcoat you wear in many performances refer to classic masculine formal dress. How did you choose this costume?

Chow: I don't see it as a persona, I don't see it as an alter ego. In terms of costume, I think this is also related to the question: Are you being performative, or are you doing a performance? I choose what feels natural to me instead of creating a "costume." It's closer to the old-school, smart, dressing-up-for-stage tradition. I won't rule out wearing a costume in the future, but this current look is more of a blank slate for my performance to happen. In my daily life, I try to avoid the camera!

Benda: Tell us how you decided on the clothes for your new digital queero. How did you choose what they wear and what hairstyle they have?

Chow: I didn't really think about the clothing; I thought about the haircut—it's my haircut. Phoenix is wearing Doc Martens (which refer to twentieth-century queer culture), a small hoop earring, and soft trousers with a version of a martial arts belt, with inspiration from Bruce Lee, the underdog (that's why people love him). The topless masculine torso is my fantasy body, and if you relate it back, it's talking about queer reality.

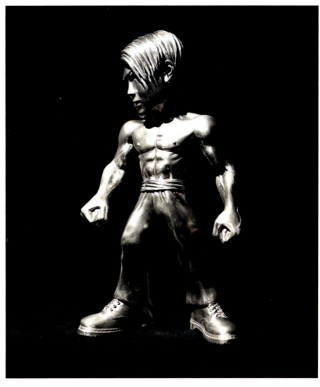

Whiskey Chow's 3D artwork of their alter ego, Phoenix Chow, 2021.

CHINESE GENDER PRONOUNS

In spoken Chinese, everyone's pronouns are "tā." In the twentieth century, written Chinese adapted to the need for gendered pronouns—he, she, and a neutral option—for translation from foreign languages.

MUXES
BELLI ROBLES MARTÍNEZ

Belli Robles Martínez is twenty-four years old, a student, a Zapotec speaker, and a small-business owner in Juchitán de Zaragoza, Oaxaca, Mexico. She is also a muxe, born a man but living as a woman and practicing traditional embroidery arts. When she sat for this interview, it was a few months before the November Vela de las Auténticas Intrépidas Buscadoras del Peligro, a celebration of centuries-old muxes and third-gender culture, where muxes wear traditional dress, often handmade. Robles Martínez describes how clothing, color, and culture are at the core of muxe life.

Benda: What is the story of the outfit you're wearing, the embroidered huipil (top) and enagua (skirt)?

Robles Martínez: I embroidered this outfit with a lot of love for myself because, as a muxe, I must arrive boldly at the celebrations in my village. Wearing it makes me feel proud of my roots and of showcasing my muxe identity, as it's well known that being muxe is synonymous with talent, or as we say here, the "grace" that characterizes us. I thank God for the life I have and for the blessing of being muxe.

Benda: How do you think your clothing reflects your inner self?

Robles Martínez: My clothing reflects my inner self through the flowers I embroider. The colors and shades fill me with joy because they're vibrant, and I always try to add my favorite colors. When I wear them, I feel full of life. My favorite colors are deep red, blue, yellow, pink, lilac, and purple.

Benda: Do you feel different when you wear traditional attire?

Robles Martínez: Completely. The outfit gives me confidence wherever I go; I feel powerful and glamorous. I love that when people see me arrive at the celebrations, they are amazed by the elegance with which I wear my attire. When I wear it, I feel like a queen—it's the symbol of my identity as a muxe and as a Zapotec.

Benda: What would you like people world-wide to know about muxes?

Robles Martínez: That we are joyful people, and we never have trouble socializing with others. They should get to know our world so we can share our life experiences and give them a little taste of our land. We are people like everyone else, and, above all, it's important to get to know people before judging them.

OPPOSITE TOP
"Zoe, Muxe with Flowers," Oaxaca, 2024, photographed by Michael Matus.

OPPOSITE BOTTOM
"Zoe, Muxe at the Stall," Oaxaca, 2024, photographed by Michael Matus.

BENDING THE RULES: FASHION BEYOND THE BINARY

HIJRAS
LAXMI NARAYAN TRIPATHI

Laxmi Narayan Tripathi is a hijra, India's third gender: born biologically male but living as a woman. Since 2014, Tripathi and a billion fellow Indian citizens have been able to choose from three gender identities on their passports: male, female, and O (transgender, intersex, nonbinary). It sounds thoroughly modern, but this striking change encodes a tradition thousands of years old; during the Mughal Empire, for example, hijras occupied high positions in government as war generals, advisors, and confidants, and more recently hijras perform religious functions in society. The 2014 right for recognition was fought for by a class of people who were still recovering from late-nineteenth-century colonial British law that labeled them criminals and degenerates. Today's hijras balance old and new. Their ancestral practices have suddenly been spotlighted as global society catches up with identities outside the binary.

Hijras often live in communal settings with a guru, receive cultural training in dance, and perform blessings at weddings. A hijra joins a gharana (community) during a reet (initiation ceremony), and thereafter she must always wear a sari. Tripathi describes wearing men's clothes—a shirt and pants—around her family to hide her identity. She changes into the sari and dupatta (a double-folded length of cloth that serves as a shawl) only when she is away from home.

Clothes, colors, jewelry, long hair, and makeup hold space in society for the hijras, as does language. Most Indian languages use gender-neutral pronouns and have names for third-gender individuals. While *hijra* is a Hindi word, the Urdu word is *khwaja sara*, the Telugu word is *napunsakudu*, and in Tamil, third-gender individuals are called *aravani*. Tripathi herself travels the world advocating for LGBTQ+ rights, and her decades-long acting, speaking, and dance career has focused on elevating the hijra role to its traditional spiritual status.

OPPOSITE
Laxmi Narayan Tripathi (in green sari, seated, center), chief of the "Kinnar Akhara" congregation for transgender people, attends evening prayers with followers during the Pitcher Festival in India, January 16, 2019.

BENDING THE RULES: FASHION BEYOND THE BINARY

"I was given two green saris, which is a ritual
that takes place when one joins the community.
They are known as jogjanam saris. I was
crowned with the community dupatta. My reet,
the christening ceremony, was thus performed
and I became a hijra. It was 1998."[4]

THE FLOWER SUIT
DAN TAULAPAPA MCMULLIN

Born in 1953 in Japan, artist Dan Taulapapa McMullin spent their early years in Samoa helping their grandmother prepare dyes for traditional Siapo hibiscus-bark textiles. Both then and today, Samoans wore the lavalava, a wraparound unisex garment anchored at the waist. Only during WWII, when American GIs outnumbered Samoans on the island, did Indigenous women in the city move the lavalava up to cover their breasts, suddenly genderizing the lavalava. The unwanted attention from Western military men was too invasive. Through the 1960s and '70s, most Samoans began wearing Western dress, meaning third-gender fa'afafine (men who live in the ways of women) and fa'afatama (women who live as men) conformed to dressing to their assigned gender rather than wearing the unisex lavalava.

Taulapapa is a fa'afafine artist, and, after training in California, they began making work within the Samoan fa'afafine culture. Their films *100 Tikis* and *Sinalela* explore Polynesian fetishization by the West, and their books *Coconut Milk* and *The Healer's Wound: A Queer Theirstory of Polynesia* tell Indigenous queer stories. Taulapapa's self-portraits plumb the different representations of who they are: a bicoastal, shorts-and-tees-wearing individual with deep ancestral ties to ancient traditions.

In Hawaiian, the term *māhū* is now understood as meaning "third gender." Puzzling over the word origin sent Taulapapa on a linguistic treasure hunt, and they searched through centuries-old Indigenous and colonial texts for clues. They found that previously *māhū* meant "steam" as well as "third gender," which suggested a connection to kahuna (healer priests) who sterilized wounds with steam (well before modern science discovered bacteria). Since third-gender individuals were often healers, the word *māhū* came to symbolize both the practice and the transgender healer performing it.

> In Samoan seiana means to decorate the self and the other
> At moments of encounter and/or celebration
> Sei were the objects of decoration
> Flowers, leaves, shells, seeds, teeth, bones, feathers[5]

Benda: Please talk about the significance of your *Auē Away* flower bodysuit activations, and how the body, the flower suit, and the choreography work together to tell the story.
Taulapapa: I originally made the bodysuits as part of a 2016 art installation; they were shown on mannequins. In 2017 they were worn in a performance by me and another poet at the Metropolitan Museum [of Art]. And in 2022 they were a part of a performance collaboration for the Hawai'i Triennial at the Honolulu Museum. This collaboration was with Kānaka 'Ōiwi Māhū transgender composer T. J. Keanu Tario and the New York/Hawai'i dance collective Te Ao Mana. The dance performance incarnation

BENDING THE RULES: FASHION BEYOND THE BINARY

Dan Taulapapa McMullin and Rosanna Raymond perform *Auē Away*, a flower suit activation in Central Park, New York City, 2017.

of *Auē Away* was based on a Samoan story of love and resurrection, from precolonial times, which was interpreted in the dance piece to music performed by Tario. At one point the dancers shed the bodysuit, revealing their bodies and skin. For me this was about change in our lives.

Benda: Are there elements of gender within the *Auē Away* suit? If so, what can the viewer take away from that?

Taulapapa: Absolutely yes. For me the suits represent a nonbinary life, where gender and sexuality are fluid and determined by one's own agency and desire and communication. In Polynesia we call the power we get from our relationships *mana*; it means that we are connected, and these connections are what give us life.

Benda: What was the process of making the suit? How did you decide on the colors, arrangement, and design?

Taulapapa: I wanted a simple triad: femme, butch, and child. The femme is green leaves, the butch is bright tropical flowers, and the child was mixed—the arrangement was intuitive. I tried to get natural-looking artificial flowers. I started by sewing them onto Lycra bodysuits but quickly realized I was too slow at this, so I switched to small safety pins. There was one instance of a performer getting stuck by a pin, but only once!

Benda: The flower suit masks the wearer's face; I am curious to know the meaning of that.

Taulapapa: I find this is part of the quality of masking traditions worldwide. Often in

Fafine, *s.* a woman.

EFFEMINATE, amio fa'afafine.

HERMAPHRODITE, *s.* faafāfine.

**fa'afā-
fine** n. Effeminate man or youth. *'O lo'o tā'a'alo fa'atasi teine ma ~:* The girls and ~ youths are playing together.

Faàfafine, a. stérile, en parlant d'une truie (barren).

Faàfafine, qui concerne les femmes (belonging to women).

Tāne, *s.* a man, a male.

tauātāne n. po. Homosexual acts between men.

TAUĀTANE, *v.* 1. to have dancing with men only. 2. To engage in fight with men, *i.e.,* brave men. TAUĀTANE, *s.* a species of sodomy, sed non introiens.

homosexual adj. (~ act): s. *tauātāne.*

that they have songs and dances of the most disgusting nature is known, so much so that I fear the most modest and chaste description of these could scarcely be made in England . . . .

FA'ATANE, *v.* to be masculine, of a woman.

Faàtane, adv. comme un homme, en parlant d'une femme (as a man).

Many immodest words excluded from the first edition have been admitted into this.

" 'Tis needful that the most immodest word
   Be looked upon and learn'd ; which, once attained,
   Comes to no further use
   But to be known and hated."

Such is my experience. Having once learnt such a word, I know how to avoid stumbling upon it in speaking. Those who take the opposite course are apt, all unconsciously, to say things which, had they known, they would have wished unsaid.

Tou te le iloa ea o e amioletonu, e le fai mo latou tofi le malo o le Atua? Aua ne'i faaeseina outou ; 'o e faitaaga, ma e ifo i tupua, ma e mulilulua, ma e tauātane, ma e faasotoma.

Mishap, mala.
Disaster, mala.
Misfortune, mala.

Mala, a. soft, as *fau mala, fu'afu'a* mala.
Mala , s. a new plantation.

Aua lua te mo-
moe ma se tane, e pei ona momoe ma se fafine ; o le mea e inosia lava lea.

Thou shalt not lie with mankinde, kinde, as with womankinde: it *is* abo-mination.

Excerpt, *The Healer's Wound: A Queer Theirstory of Polynesia*, Dan Taulapapa McMullin.

religious ceremonies (I am myself a con-firmed atheist with a fascination for reli-gions), people wear masks and overall body costumes to take on the spirit of something greater than themselves—or, one might say, an aspect of themself that doesn't otherwise come through. For the audience (or the congregation), this disguise enables them to accept the performer as another being that is being represented.

Benda: Is there anything you would like to make sure the reader understands about Polynesian gender identity?
Taulapapa: I think Polynesian gender identity is as heteronormative in Polynesia as anywhere else. However, in Polynesia—because of our ancient pre-Christian

religion—those who are nonbinary, who step outside of the heteronormative, are seen as a vital part of the community, because they live in various worlds and facilitate communication between those worlds (between male and female, between earthly and spiritual, life and death, knowledge and chaos).

HAWAIIAN DRAG CLUBS
I AM A BOY

In contemporary Honolulu, it would be inconceivable that a male drag performer would be required by Hawaiian law to wear an "I Am a Boy" pin on their chest. But a 1963 ruling meant that female impersonators at the Glade Show Club in the city's Chinatown district had to identify themselves with a bright red pin like that shown here. While the original pins simply read "I Am a Boy," subsequent pins added the name, address, and sometimes photos of the Glade performers, thus subverting the message and grabbing free advertising by pointing customers to the shows.[6]

Until the law was repealed in 1972, drag performers were harassed, beaten, and denied basic rights, despite the joyful popularity of the Glade and its famous performers like Prince Hanalei. The club closed in 1982, leaving behind a twenty-year legacy of early drag history. In 2023, Sasha Colby celebrated a capstone to that history, becoming the first native-Hawaiian competitor to win *RuPaul's Drag Race*.

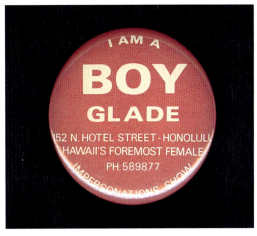

"I Am a Boy" pin, Queer Music Archives, undated.

JEMIMA WILKINSON
THE UNIVERSAL FRIEND

Somewhere near a house in Jerusalem, in Upstate New York, is the final resting place of a traveling gender trailblazer. This is no modern grave or modern house. It's a two-hundred-year-old, white, wood-clad home with the nonbinary body of a preacher and prophetess buried nearby. No one knows the exact location of the grave anymore. Loyal followers who moved the corpse of the Friend, as they were known, swore an oath of secrecy.

In life and death, the Friend's body and identity were a battleground in a country that itself was a battleground for its identity as a new nation. Born in Rhode Island in 1752 as a woman, Jemima Wilkinson shed their birth gender in 1776 following a life-threatening fever and afterward would only answer to the name the Universal Friend or the Friend. They were convinced that they had been reborn as the Christian Holy Spirit.

The Friend used clothing to create a unique visual identity that aligned with their rejection of the binary. Townspeople walking the same cobbled streets as the Friend would have seen a solemnly dressed individual in combined male and female colonial dress: a dark robe of modest fabric (worn with a plain undergarment), a man's

"A part of her pride consisted in dressing after a fashion entirely her own, which resembled neither that of men nor women. She wore an undergarment with long sleeves, wristbands and collar, and a large cravat about her neck—petticoat and slippers; a vest cut sloping to the right and left from the centre, a kind of coatee dress similar to a lady's riding habit, the upper part buttoned, and cut sloping below, so as to show the edges of her vest, and over the whole a long robe of black silk or white satin; and in public she always appeared with a huge black beaver turned down at the sides and tied under her chin with a ribbon. She wore no head dress, having her fine black hair combed and dressed in several sets of curls and ringlets...she had the appearance of a personage of no ordinary character."[7]

Oil on canvas portrait of the Public Universal Friend by John Lee Douglas "J.L.D." Mathies, completed in 1816.

white cravat layered with a women's white kerchief, a petticoat, soft shoes, and a masculine cape. The Friend's hair was neatly dressed—slightly longer than contemporary male styles, but more modest than female styles—and they didn't wear a bonnet or cover their hair in the feminine fashion of the time. Instead, they wore a masculine, Quaker-style, wide-brimmed, beaver fur hat.

The Friend's identity extended past clothes to all aspects of their visual communication: they had the initials "U.F." emblazoned on the side of their carriage and luggage and the initials "I.H.S." (Iesus Hominum Salvator, meaning Jesus Savior of Men) on their linens. There is only one engraving and one painting of the Friend that survive. Nevertheless, the Friend spread messages of religious tolerance and piety (without the use of the internet, social media, or photography).

As their dress would have been puzzling to many people, so were their pronouns, as the English language was ill equipped for nonbinary people. Contemporary (but controversial) writer David Hudson published *Memoir of a Prophetess* in 1821, noting how followers wrestled with how to address the Friend:

> Having assumed the title of "Universal Friend of mankind," she had no further occasion for the name Jemima Wilkinson; accordingly all her followers were taught as a duty to consider and call her the "Universal Friend," and on all occasions abstain from speaking of her in such a manner as to indicate any

distinction of sex....[They] would never say her or hers, though to avoid it they might be compelled to use the word "Friend" a hundred times in the same conversation.[8]

Two centuries later, English speakers are still grappling with a language that falls short of encompassing all genders, and the quest to get it right is all too relatable. The Yates County Historical Society currently uses "they/them" pronouns for the Friend, while twenty-first-century biographers Paul B. Moyer and Herbert A. Wisbey alternate between "he/him" and "she/her" in their books.[9]

THE BATTLE OF THE ROSEBUD
OSCH-TISCH AND THE OTHER MAGPIE

"The woman, I remember, wore a stuffed woodpecker on her head, and her forehead was painted yellow."[10] This is how Pretty Shield, a seventy-year-old Crow medicine woman, described the warrior The Other Magpie to Frank B. Linderman. Linderman—a cowboy, hunter, and trapper—gained the trust of the Crow tribe in Montana and captured Pretty Shield's oral history in his 1932 book *Red Mother*. Recounting the 1867 Battle of the Rosebud in the Black Mountains of Montana, Pretty Shield detailed how an unusual pair of gender-nonconforming Crow warriors rode with US troops and Shoshone scouts against the Cheyenne, Sioux, and Lakota tribes. She described how the two warriors—The Other Magpie and Osch-Tisch (also known as Finds-them-and-kills-them)—did not expect to return from battle: "Both these women expected death that day. Finds-them-and-kills-them, afraid to have the [Lakota] find her dead with woman-clothing on her, changed them to a man's before fighting commenced."[11]

When Osch-Tisch survived and returned from the Rosebud, they would have changed out of their men's battle dress and resumed wearing women's dress, as they had their entire adult life. They were born biologically male, but they were living as a woman. The Other Magpie, who was born biologically female, similarly chose men's dress in battle to avoid scrutiny but wore men's and women's dress in their daily life.

Osch-Tisch was a Two-Spirit individual, or bòte, and occupied a gender role that matched their clothing. As Christian Allaire, fashion and style writer at *Vogue*, observes,

> The North American Indigenous community traditionally honors its Two-Spirit people, a term associated with Indigenous people possessing both male and female spirits. Fulfilling both gender roles in their personal life, and during ceremonies, Two-Spirits are regarded with respect as they have a special ability to exist between both worlds. Today, being Two-Spirit is also an umbrella term, representing Indigenous queer people at large.[12]

Osch-Tisch and The Other Magpie appear in the undated photograph on page 203, taken by John H. Fouch—the earliest-known photograph of a Two-Spirit person. Historian James Brust told me, "I believe [Fouch] didn't take the photo because of their gender, but because of their bravery in battle."[14] In the 1870s, frontiersmen ventured West with stereo-cameras (new post–Civil War technology) to capture magnificent scenery. Along the way they also took hundreds of portraits of Native American individuals, white settlers, and cowboys.

"**Yes, a Crow woman fought with Three-Stars on the Rosebud, two of them did, for that matter; but one of them was neither a man nor a woman. She looked like a man, and yet she wore woman's clothing; and she had the heart of a woman. Besides, she did women's work. Her name was Finds-them-and-kills-them. She was not a man, yet not a woman....She was not as strong as a man, and yet she was wiser than a woman....The other woman... was a wild one who had no man of her own. She was bad and brave, this one. Her name was The-other-magpie; and she was pretty.**"[13]

In Fouch's photograph, Osch-Tisch wears a woman's cloth dress. Typically made from government-issued printed cotton fabric, cloth dresses had wide neck holes, wide sleeves, and full ankle-length skirts. They were transitional clothes, bridging the gap between traditional Crow dress and early-twentieth-century Western frontier dress. Osch-Tisch wears traditional, hand-made, single-skin, side-seam, hide moccasins, which were molded to their foot during wear. As a master of building lodges from buffalo skins, Osch-Tisch knew how to catch, skin, tan, bleach, and paint animal hides from deer, mountain goat, elk, mountain sheep, and antelope.

The Other Magpie wears a man's shirt—two skins joined together with leather thongs—and tall moccasins meant for riding horses. Crow men would have worn a knee-length hide shirt, later switching to waist-length shirts with leggings. The Other Magpie wears a woolen blanket robe over both shoulders, in men's fashion, rather than over one shoulder, as in women's fashion.

Osch-Tisch lived until the late 1920s, long enough to see their tribe moved to a reservation. It is likely that they were persecuted by missionaries and government officials spurred by Christianity to renounce their identity for a male gender. US Army General Hugh Scott interviewed Osch-Tisch late in life and documented the highly decorative regalia they had crafted for their own burial. It was a two-skin women's cloth dress adorned with precious abalone shells, accompanied by a woman's beaded belt. Without careful understanding of Indigenous dress, Two-Spirit identity, and cultural context, the powerful story of Osch-Tisch and The Other Magpie might have otherwise been overlooked.

OPPOSITE
Warriors Osch-Tisch and The Other Magpie, 1877, Crow Nation.

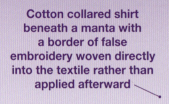

Cotton collared shirt beneath a manta with a border of false embroidery woven directly into the textile rather than applied afterward

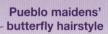

Pueblo maidens' butterfly hairstyle

Iconic Zuni silver squash blossom necklace and hoop earrings

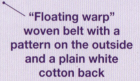

"Floating warp" woven belt with a pattern on the outside and a plain white cotton back

Folded-over deerskin boots, which could be pulled above the knee for horseback riding

WE'WHA

While Osch-Tisch and The Other Magpie adjusted to life on reservations, We'wha, a Zuni Two-Spirit master potter from New Mexico, was adjusting to life in Washington, DC, as a tribal cultural ambassador. We'wha, born in 1849, had been a male-bodied Lachmana (the Zuni word for Two-Spirit individuals) artist living as a woman for more than thirty years when they met President Grover Cleveland at the White House in 1885 or 1886. We'wha was accompanied by close friend and ethnographer Matilda Coxe Stevenson, who organized the cultural visit to raise the profile of Indigenous tribes in America. The two remained close companions until We'wha's death in 1896.

An 1886 article in the *National Tribune* says of We'wha, "Her sacred white cotton blanket was so arranged as to form a drapery from her shoulders nearly to her feet, covering one shoulder and leaving the other shoulder and arm entirely bare in a purely classic style."[15] The article describes them as a woman, but Zuni thoughts on gender are shaped in part by what skills a person perfects. According to scholar Will Roscoe, "The social roles of men and women were not biologically determined but acquired through life experience and shaped through a series of initiations....Individuals were born 'raw.' To become useful adults, they had to be 'cooked.' For the Zunis, gender was part of being 'cooked'—a social construction."[16]

According to the *National Tribune*, gender-specific skills played a role in We'wha's time in Washington. They learned to knit there, as knitting would have been considered a settler woman's skill in the city. But they refused to partake of the skill until after they returned home because weaving was considered a man's trade. While they were in Washington, they were "particular in not wishing to do anything which is considered distinctively masculine among her people, and in avoiding a style of dress peculiar to men." The article went on to say that they were

dressed in a dark, blue-striped, short skirt of a material and pattern resembling seersucker, a loose shirtwaist of white cotton, and over her shoulders a sacred blanket made by Indians. Moccasins enveloped her legs and feet, and each moccasin required a whole buckskin to make it, but only one corner of it was used to cover each foot, the remainder being wrapped about the ankle and calf of the leg....Her head was bare, but while in the street she carried over it a big red satin parasol, which she purchased in Washington....Around her neck she had an immense necklace of silver beads and a silver crescent as a pendant, all made by native workmen in Zuni.[17]

若衆: WAKASHŪ

The streets of seventeenth-century Edo (Tokyo), Japan, were alive with the fluttering sleeves of furisodes (long-sleeved kimonos) and clacking wooden geta (sandals). Dark pine buildings with shoji rice paper doors hid laughter and chatter, amorous encounters, and thoughtful debates. Pleasure, leisure, and learning were closely related in this bustling city. While some courtesans paired their furisodes with voluminous obis and fans, others tucked an o-tanto katana (sword) at their waist, suggestive of their pending manhood.

The son of an affluent lord and the son of a struggling farmer in the Edo period might have both experienced the adolescent metamorphosis of a wakashū, even if the circumstances that led them to this transitional gender were of two separate worlds. Like many classical societies, Japanese culture practiced a coming of age for young men that included a social and sexual apprenticeship under older men, a pederastic practice known as shudō. This era of their lives was fluid, neither man nor boy nor woman, though assuming aspects of all of them.

Wakashū were so famous for their youthful, fluid beauty that many people simply called them maegami (youth itself). But in Japan boyhood wasn't necessarily dictated by the march of time. The concept of age was tied to gender through a man's choice of whether to shirk boyhood or not. In the West, a man might gain the ability to grow a beard, and therefore be seen as having reached adulthood, but young men shaved their hair to signify maturity.[18] That determined how society interpreted age and gender. A wakashū stepped out of their identity and transformed into a man by choosing to shave their maegami.

The Edo period's transitional gender effectively ended at the end of the Meiji period in 1868. Wakashū were marginalized by new government laws punishing cross-dressing. As authorities enforced short hair for men, mandatory haircuts meant wakashū lost the physical symbol of their identity and became invisible in modern Japanese culture.

PRONOUNS

Japanese gender pronouns were neutral, with all people referred to as *kare*, until the end of the Meiji period in 1912, when Japan opened to the West.

WIVES OF THE GODS

Giovanni Antonio Cavazzi, a Capuchin missionary priest, was fascinated by the swirling shiver of bells and leaves, of music and feet pounding into the iron-rich soil, as he wrote his account of the Ganga-Ya-Chibanda—high priest of the Giagues—in Angola in 1687. Cavazzi was confused by the shaman, a man who "dresses ordinarily as a woman and makes an honor of being called the Grandmother."[19] Ganga-Ya-Chibanda was a jinbandaa, a third gender that was widespread across African cultures. Jinbandaa had a transient gender identity and were therefore seen as being transient spirits that could bridge birth, life, and death.

One of the only surviving primary images of a jinbandaa is an illustration by Giovanni Antonio Cavazzi during his mission to Angola from 1665 to 1668, in which he saw the Ganga-Ya-Chibanda.[20] This jinbandaa is dressed in daily women's dress with carefully arranged lengths of cloth wrapped as a skirt and tunic. The rag at the waist is a breech-clout, which would have been worn by men. Whether this is a signifier of the jinbandaa gender is unknown but does explain the undyed cloth and indigo patina in Cavazzi's depiction. If the garment was originally worn beneath the jinbandaa's skirt, the skirt's blue dye likely would have rubbed off in the humidity and heat.

When the jinbandaa were swept up and displaced by the slave trade, much of their identity was dismantled to fit into Christian frameworks. When one Beninese jinbandaa named Antônio or Vitória in Brazil was asked

Giovanni Antonio Cavazzi wrote his "Missione Evangelica al Regno del Congo" manuscript detailing Angolan life in the seventeenth century, and made this sketch of a jinbandaa priest, which inspired the digital color rendering opposite.

to wear slave dress, he insisted on choosing his own combination of clothes, much like the sketch on page 210, which is based on written descriptions of enslaved jinbandaa. Author James H. Sweet recounts, "Refusing to wear the clothes that his master gave him, Antônio instead chose to dress in a white waist jacket buttoned down the front, with a vest made from an old woolen cloth that he found in his master's stables. On his head, he wore a tightly wrapped white linen, topped off by a hat." While many of Antônio/Vitória's gestures were feminine, "he was also observed removing his hat and bowing 'like a man.'"[21]

This connection between a spiritual gender, power, and costume continues today in places like Yorubaland, where possession priests for the Orixá (a pantheon of West

BENDING THE RULES: FASHION BEYOND THE BINARY

One of the only surviving primary images of a jinbandaa individual is the manuscript sketch opposite. Though the names of the garments are unknown, careful consideration went into the arrangement of rectangular lengths of fabrics in this illustration. The tunic is wrapped beneath one arm and pinned at the shoulders, allowing fabric to cascade down one side only and maintain a narrower fit. The cloth at the waist might also be a breechclout worn over the skirt to dry one's hands or signify a mixture of gendered garments. The turban is key in the jinbandaa's ensemble, as spiritual power is centered in the head.

African Gods) dress as women regardless of their biological sex because they believe feminine energy opens them up to the Gods. These priests are called wives of the Gods, regardless of their personal gender identity. They take on women's professions and wear women's clothing, jewelry, and makeup. "Yet these male possession priests are never

This sketch is based on descriptions of enslaved jinbandaa individuals in Brazil and put to trial during the Inquisition for sodomy.

viewed as anything other than 'men,'" writes Sweet. "They signal their spiritual personas and ritual power through female gesture and dress."[22]

THAILAND GENDERS

FEMALE DRESS

typical female dress	(Straight) Female	a woman attracted to men
typical female dress	Dee	a woman attracted to manly women, Toms
typical female dress	Gay Queen	a womanly man attracted to men
typical female dress	Tom Gay Queen	a womanly Tom attracted to Toms
typical female dress	Kathoey/Ladyboy	a man who wants to be a woman
typical female dress	Angee	a Kathoey who likes Toms

MALE DRESS

typical male dress	(Straight) Male	a man attracted to women
typical male dress	Tom Gay King	a manly Tom attracted to Toms
typical male dress	Boat	a man attracted to women, Gay Kings, Gay Queens (but not Ladyboys)
typical male dress	Gay King	a manly man who likes men

NONBINARY DRESS

tomboy dress	Tom	a woman attracted to women, Dees
tomboy dress	Tom Gay	a woman attracted to women, Toms, Dees
typical female dress	Bi(sexual)	a woman attracted to Bi, Toms, lesbians, men
typical male dress	Tom Gay Two-Way	a Tom who is either a Tom Gay King or Tom Gay Queen
tomboy dress	Lesbian	a woman who likes women
typical male dress	Adam	a man who likes Toms
typical male dress	Cherry	a woman who likes gay men, Kathoey
all options of dress	Samyaan	a woman who likes Toms, lesbians, and women, and can also be any of them

AFTERWORD

∞ (INFINITY)

Eva & Adele at the 2018 Hirshhorn Spring Gala, wearing matching ensembles.

The three artists in this section—the duo Eva & Adele, Nayland Blake, and Richard Gallo—have been working in the space of self-expression and gender identity since the 1970s and '80s, laying the aesthetic groundwork for the twenty-first-century gender-identity revolution. Within their daily public performance practice, Eva & Adele ask us to question why and how we use fashion. Nayland Blake, because of their fashion activism in gallery and museum spaces, asks us to look at modern masculinity and how it can expand. And Richard Gallo turned every space he occupied into a performance stage; with his outlandish costumes, he asked mainstream passersby to question why they chose to conform to the binary through everyday dress. Through these trailblazers, we can more clearly see the infinite combinations of self.

EVE & ADELE

In 2018, New Yorkers were treated to the joyful sight of German artists Eva & Adele in matching red party dresses; white sashes with red crystal, lip-shaped brooches; demure white Mary Jane pumps; and elaborate makeup. Photographer Nicole Gnesa, who snapped Eva & Adele that evening, describes how the looks came together: "Eva & Adele told me that the brooches are by Salvador Dalí from the Dalí Museum, and the dresses were customized for Eva & Adele by fashion designer Isabel Vollrath in Berlin."[1] Eva & Adele sometimes work with fashion designers and stylists. But usually, they create their own look and travel with multiple suitcases of carefully planned, matching ensembles.

Eva & Adele explain, "We are both dandies and monks."[2] In their studio in Germany, they work like monks, meticulously and methodically, to create their dual image and the photographs, artworks, and mixed media that go with it. In the street, perhaps at a bus stop, they define dandyism with their matching looks. The artists describe how they are not looking inward or back; they look forward to what is to come: "We had to find a new word in addition to art and we came up

with 'futuring'—to create the future and to focus on something that will happen in the future. We became a symbol of bringing gender into the future, we are a new gender."[3]

NAYLAND BLAKE

A lover of fashion, animal costumes, skirts for men, and Japanese avant-garde design, Nayland Blake is an artist, writer, educator, and curator who uses their daily sartorial choices to celebrate self-expression. Born into the vibrant counterculture of 1960s New York City, they studied at Bard College and then California Institute of the Arts, where a woman's prom dress was their graduation look to receive their MFA diploma. From 2019 to 2021, a touring retrospective of their work, *No Wrong Holes*, journeyed from Los Angeles to Cambridge, Massachusetts. Artists from San Francisco and New York influenced their love of city spaces as theatrical backdrops. Blake remembers performance artist Leigh Bowery and drag queen Ms. Colombia embracing New York club life as a safe zone for gender-expansive individuals, and folks making a living in Times Square as characters and buskers.

Blake's three looks shown here are energized by a femme/butch duality. The recipe includes tulle skirts, blazers, smock dresses, beard accessories, leather boots, bowler hats, bags, bright socks, brogues, animal horns, and plenty of color. Their beard bows and braids are an homage to the Shaggy Man from *The World of Oz* children's books.

LEFT
Baring their midriff, Blake wears a black net top, black bra and wide ruched skirt, topped with a horned bonnet.

MIDDLE
Blake's 2022 Whitney Biennial Opening look, with blazer by JCRT, market stall–patterned skirt, and orange beard bows.

RIGHT
A black skirt with a gray tulle petticoat is the centerpiece for this Blake outfit, finished off with beard braids and a tall black hat.

At the Whitney Biennial on June 9, 2022, Blake hosted a Gender Discard Party where visitors could bring an article of gendered clothing, tell the story of the item, and perhaps pick up a new item discarded by someone else. The party was an opportunity for people to speak in public about their relationship to gender identity. Someone left a bridesmaid's dress, while another dropped off classic men's boxer shorts. Blake's art and life blend together through self-portraits, photographs, and a daily catwalk of fashion, textiles, accessories, and adornments.

In this ca. 1970 black-and-white photograph by Robert Ippolito, Richard Gallo plays the character Mr. Bold, using New York City's Grand Army Plaza as his stage and passersby as his audience.

RICHARD GALLO

Imagine sitting in New York's Grand Army Plaza in the 1970s and seeing a figure in a red tailcoat, combat boots, green wig, chicken wire, and a hundred-yard-long trail of tulle coming toward you. Because of the layers of costume and disguise, it would be hard to tell that the figure was late-twentieth-century, New York–based, queer performance artist Richard Gallo—it could be any body of any gender identity. An eyewitness noted that "Richard performed without speaking…he would cross the loosely defined line between the audience and the performance space and joined the viewers seated on the benches—commiserated and placed clothespins on their lapels. The audience would roar with delight."[4]

Playing with costumes (fetish corsets, military airmen's boots, leopard and zebra prints, capes made from moving blankets, rubber waders, and fishnet bodysuits, to name a few) meant playing with gender identity. Mixing masculine and feminine pieces worked perfectly in a theatrical space. Gallo described his mischievous aesthetic process: "The costumes were a natural thing. I've done it since Pratt. When we were there, B.W. [theater director Robert Wilson] and I would take turns trying to top each other. He would do a piece and say, 'Everyone wear khaki.' I would show up in a red tux with two hundred yards of red chiffon."[5]

"I would not be doing justice to the future of clothes if I did not point out that practically all psychologists who have bothered to consider the subject agree that eventually we will all become nudists."[6]

ACKNOWLEDGMENTS

I hope this book plays a small part in celebrating the beautiful kaleidoscope of fashion, textiles, and adornments that are a catalyst for self-expression. This book is dedicated to the scholars who brought the history of clothing and gender identity to life, from the 1950s onward, for future generations to build upon: Jo B. Paoletti, Claudia Brush Kidwell, Christian Allaire, Joanne B. Eicher, Elizabeth Wayland Barber, Alok Vaid-Menon, Valerie Steele, Kit Heyam, and Anne Hollander.

This book also honors the power of the new generation, first and foremost my daughter Mina Elam and my niece Mira Achilles. My brilliant research assistant on this book, Ashley Kae Snyder, shared many insights on how to think beyond the binary. My students at CalArts teach me every day about what comes next and how to talk about it. In my role as a costume designer, I have the privilege of working with young actors and creative team members who actively make new spaces in the world for self-expression. They and many others will lead the way with grace and clarity.

Some of the original photographs and illustrations in this book were made possible through a 2024 California Institute of the Arts Development Grant and the 2022 CalArts Provost's Research and Practice Fellowship in Equity, Diversity, and Inclusivity. Gwyn Conaway and I are extremely grateful for their support. Thank you to the Seattle Art Museum, the Burke Museum, National Museums Scotland, National Museums of Ireland, the Fashion Institute of Design and Merchandising Museum Collections (special thanks to Kevin Jones and Christina Johnson), and the Dress and Textile Collections at the Los Angeles County Museum of Art (special thanks to Clarissa Esguerra) for opening their wondrous archives to us. They are the guardians of treasures.

This book brought people across the globe together in conversation. I would like to thank Michael Matus Gomez for his help sharing the muxes traditions in Mexico, Minjee Kim for her detailed insights into Korean dress, Mo Khoja for his help with Saudi Arabian clothing, and Jim Brust for his academic work on African history and customs.

Endless thanks go to Jennifer Thompson, executive editor at PA Press; managing editor Sara Stemen; and designer Natalie Snodgrass for their beautiful work bringing this book to life, and to my literary agent, Leigh Eisenman, who championed this book from its inception to the very end.

Finally, I would like to thank my parents, Miroslav and Helena Benda, and my brother, Cyril Benda, for their support, and of course my very talented husband, Mike Elam, who took up the slack while I wrote this book as he did his own demanding full-time industrial design job. While folding laundry recently, he picked up our tween daughter's gray, pleated, knee-length, kilt-like skirt and said, "I might just kind of want to wear something like this…" May this book inspire us all to play!

NOTES

INTRODUCTION

1 Qween Jean, in discussion with the author, August 19, 2024. Additional quotes are taken from this interview.
2 Michael Sylvan Robinson, in discussion with the author, October 4, 2024.
3 Charles Fréger, in discussion with the author, May 10, 2024.

NEUTRALITY

1 Chloe Chapin, in discussion with the author, September 24, 2024.
2 "Flesh Kimono, Jon Eric Riis," The Chung Young Yang Embroidery Museum, Sookmyung Women's University, Seoul, South Korea, https://artsandculture.google.com/asset/flesh-kimono-jon-eric-riis/ewEXul5oJBLT2g?hl=en.
3 Mel Brittner Wells, email message to author, September 19, 2024.
4 Nicole Phelps, "Introducing Altu, a New Collection of Genderful Fashion from Joseph Altuzarra," *Vogue*, December 21, 2021, https://www.vogue.com/article/altu-genderful-collection-joseph-altuzarra.
5 Phelps, "Introducing Altu."
6 Alexander Fury, "The Lighter Side of Rick Owens," *New York Times*, March 2, 2017, https://www.nytimes.com/2017/03/02/t-magazine/rick-owens-fashion-designer.html.
7 Leona Liu, "Rick Owens on Improvising During Covid-19, Gender-Bending Style and How He Learned to Appreciate the Brand Collaboration Interview," *Style*, November 23, 2021, https://www.scmp.com/magazines/style/luxury/article/3157115/rick-owens-fashions-lord-darkness-improvising-during-covid?module=perpetual_scroll_0&pgtype=article.
8 Fury, "The Lighter Side of Rick Owens."
9 Bernhard Willhelm, in discussion with the author, July 27, 2024.
10 Jawni Han, "Issey Miyake Was Armor for My Changing Body," *The Cut*, November 7, 2023, https://www.thecut.com/article/issey-miyake-pleats-please-trans-identity.html.
11 Alexandra Harney, "The Herbivore's Dilemma," *Slate*, June 15, 2009, https://slate.com/news-and-politics/2009/06/japan-panics-about-the-rise-of-herbivores-young-men-who-shun-sex-don-t-spend-money-and-like-taking-walks.html.

12 Kelly Ruiz, email message to the author, November 2, 2024.
13 Leslie Reinhardt, "Serious Daughters: Dolls, Dress, and Female Virtue in the Eighteenth Century," *American Art* 20, no. 2 (2006): 33–34, https://doi.org/10.1086/507499.
14 J. Adams Puffer, *The Boy and His Gang* (Riverside Press, 1912), 74–75.
15 Jo B. Paoletti, *Sex and Unisex: Fashion, Feminism, and the Sexual Revolution* (Indiana University Press, 2015), 95–97.
16 Bernhard Diensberg, "The Etymology of Modern English 'Girl': An Old Problem Reconsidered." Neuphilologische Mitteilungen 85 (4): 473–75 (1984). https://jstor.org/stable/43343623
17 Sally Potter, message to the author, September 25, 2024.
18 Esther MacCallum-Stewart and Jude Roberts, eds., *Gender and Sexuality in Contemporary Popular Fantasy: Beyond Boy Wizards and Kick-Ass Chicks* (Routledge, 2016), 2.
19 Russell W. Belk, "Extended Self in a Digital World: Table 1," *Journal of Consumer Research* 40, no. 3 (2013): 477–500. https://doi.org/10.1086/671052.
20 Elizabeth Hawes, *Why Is a Dress?* (Viking, 1942).
21 Michael Maier, *Symbola aureae mensae* (1617), chapter 6.
22 Cassius Dio, *The Collected Works of Cassius Dio*, trans. Herbert Baldwin Foster (Halcyon, 2010), Book 79.
23 Richard Hunter, *Plato's Symposium* (Oxford University Press, 2004), 123.
24 Plato, *The Symposium*, trans. Benjamin Jowett (New York Pocket Library, 1950), 13.
25 Minjee Kim, in discussion with the author, May 14, 2024.

UNISEX

1 Minjee Kim, in discussion with the author, May 14, 2024.
2 Jo B. Paoletti, in discussion with the author, September 18, 2024.
3 Paoletti, *Sex and Unisex*, 120.
4 Paoletti, *Sex and Unisex*, 89.
5 Paoletti, in discussion with the author, September 18, 2024.
6 Paoletti, in discussion with the author, September 18, 2024.

7   Paoletti, in discussion with the author, September 18, 2024.

8   Katie Clark Blakesley, "'A Style of Our Own': Modesty and Mormon Women, 1951–2008," *Dialogue: A Journal of Mormon Thought* 42, no. 2 (Summer 2009): 32.

9   Rory Scanlon, in discussion with the author, May 27, 2023.

10 Margaret Toscano, in discussion with the author, May 26, 2023.

11 Paoletti, in discussion with the author, September 18, 2024.

12 From archive research at the Arizona State University Fashion Institute of Design and Merchandising, Rudi Gernreich Archives, September 21, 2023.

13 Thayaht & RAM Archive, 2018, Florence, Italy, https://www.thayaht-ram.com.

14 Archive Research, Seattle Art Museum, courtesy of Pam McClusky, June 29, 2022.

BINARY

1   *Ladies Home Journal*, February 1918, 98, https://babel.hathitrust.org/cgi/pt?id=mdp.39015018013220&seq=186.

2   Troy Morgan, in discussion with the author, November 1, 2024.

3   Annette Becker, email to author, June 29, 2023.

4   Theodore H. White, "For President Kennedy: An Epilogue," *Life*, December 6, 1963.

5   Elizabeth Way, *Ann Lowe: American Couturier* (Rizzoli, 2023), 175.

6   https://scholarworks.uni.edu/suffrage_images/.

7   https://scalar.usc.edu/works/suffrage-on-display/dunston-weiler-lithograph-suffragette-series.

8   J. C. Flügel, *The Psychology of Clothes* (Hogarth Press & The Institute of Psycho-Analysis, 1930), 110.

9   Louis-Sébastien Mercier, *Tableau de Paris*, vol. 11–12 (Legare Street Press, 2023), 86.

10 Paul Poiret, *My First 50 Years* (Victor Gollancz, 1931), 72–73.

11 Robin R. Wang, "Dong Zhongshu's Transformation of Yin-Yang Theory and Contesting of Gender Identity," *Philosophy East and West* 55, no. 2 (2005): 209–31, https://doi.org/10.1353/pew.2005.0013.

12 Chungbae Kim, *Peonies: The Flowers of Peace and Prosperity* (National Palace Museum of Korea, 2021), 115–37.

13 Jean Paul Gaultier, Paris, France, 1985.

14 Rosalind Jana, "14 of Jean Paul Gaultier's Greatest Runway Moments," *Vogue France*, April 24, 2020, https://www.vogue.fr/fashion/article/14-of-jean-paul-gaultiers-greatest-runway-moments.

15 Elizabeth Hawes, *Fashion Is Spinach* (Random House, 1938), 297.

SINGULAR

1   Janelle Monáe, "PYNK," music video, songwriters: Janelle Robinson, Claire Boucher, Taylor Parks, Nathanial Irvin III, Charles Joseph II, Wynne Bennett, Steven Tyler, Glen Ballard, and Richard Goodman, directed by Emma Westenberg, 2018.

2   Mark Bryan, in discussion with the author, July 21, 2023.

3   Tshepo Mokoena, "Caster Semenya: 'How Would I Label Myself? I'm an African. I'm a Woman. I'm a Different Woman,'" *Guardian* (US edition), October 28, 2023, https://www.theguardian.com/sport/2023/oct/28/athlete-caster-semenya-interview-im-a-woman-im-a-different-woman.

4   Kate Adie, *Corsets to Camouflage: Women and War* (Hachette UK, 2004), ix.

5   Cally Blackman, *One Hundred Years of Menswear* (Laurence King, 2009), 5.

6   Frederic A. Birmingham, ed., *Esquire Fashion Guide for All Occasions* (Harper & Brothers, 1957), 8.

7   CULTURESHOP, "Japan's Masculinity in Motion," July 21, 2015, https://medium.com/@Quantum Singapore/japan-s-masculinity-crisis-the-rise-of-the-herbivore-man-56a6569a0e3f.

8   Dian Hanson, *The Little Book of Tom of Finland: Cops & Robbers* (Taschen, 2016), 192.

9   *Tom of Finland: The Art of Pleasure* (Taschen, 1992), 13.

10 Holly George-Warren and Michelle Freedman, *How the West Was Worn* (Harry N. Abrams, 2001); William Manns and Elizabeth Clair Flood, *Cowboys & the Trappings of the Old West* (Zon International, 1997).

11 E. C. "Teddy Blue" Abbott and Helena Huntington Smith, *We Pointed Them North: Recollections of a Cowpuncher* (University of Oklahoma Press, 1939), 40.

12 Abbott and Smith, *We Pointed Them North*, 207.

13 Abbott and Smith, *We Pointed Them North*, 107.

14 Kenneth Bamberg, in discussion with Gwyn Conaway, November 23, 2024.

15 Thomas Vinciguerra, "The Bunny Is Back," *Wall Street Journal*, August 27, 2011.

16 Gloria Steinem, "A Bunny's Tale I & II," *Show*, May 1, 1962, and June 1, 1963, https://undercover.hosting.nyu.edu/s/undercover-reporting/item-set/61.

17 Messy Nessy, "Bedtime Reading: The 1960 Official Playboy Club Manual," Messy Nessy Chic, August 6, 2021, https://www.messynessychic.com/2012/07/03/bedtime-reading-the-1960-official-playboy-club-bunny-manual/.

18 Bretman Rock, *You're That Bitch: & Other Cute Lessons About Being Unapologetically Yourself* (Harper Collins, 2023), 75

19 Rock, *You're That Bitch*, xi.

20 Carolyn A. Day, *Consumptive Chic: A History of Beauty, Fashion, and Disease* (Bloomsbury Academic, 2017), 85.

21 Gail Chin, "The Gender of Buddhist Truth: The Female Corpse in a Group of Japanese Paintings," *Japanese Journal of Religious Studies* 25, no. 3/4 (1998): 277–317, https://doi.org/10.18874/jjrs.25.3-4.1998.277-317.

22 Instagram post, Maison Margiela (@maisonmargiela), February 1, 2024.

23 Instagram post, Maison Margiela (@maisonmargiela), February 1, 2024.

24 Instagram post, Maison Margiela (@maisonmargiela), February 1, 2024.

25 Instagram post, Maison Margiela (@maisonmargiela), February 6, 2024.

26 Bliss Foster, "The Kafkaesque Couture of Thom Browne," posted August 21, 2023, YouTube, 16:35 min., https://www.youtube.com/watch?v=7Xdo1iJfU8w.

DUALITY

1 Grayson Perry, *The Descent of Man* (Penguin, 2017), 63.

2 Cady Lang, "'You Must Wear the Clothes, the Clothes Must Not Wear You.' Let Billy Porter and His Stylist Explain the Story Behind His Buzzy Fashion Statements," *Time*, January 6, 2020, https://time.com/5759620/billy-porter-stylist-sam-ratelle-interview/.

3 Lang, "'You Must Wear the Clothes."

4 Inscription on anatomical drawing published by Charles Turner, June 14, 1810, https://www.britishmuseum.org/collection/object/P_1868-0808-7947.

5 The New York State Senate, legislation, April 26, 2024, https://www.nysenate.gov/legislation/laws/PEN/P3TNA240.

6 Hugh Ryan, "How Dressing in Drag Was Labeled a Crime in the 20th Century," History, September 14, 2023, https://www.history.com/news/stonewall-riots-lgbtq-drag-three-article-rule.

7 "Grayson Perry," Pål Hansen, February 21, 2019, https://www.palhansen.com/latestblogposts/2019/2/21/grayson-perry.

8 Belle Hutton, "Artist Grayson Perry: 'I Describe Myself as "Gender Rigid,"'" *AnOther*, April 18, 2019, https://www.anothermag.com/art-photography/11658/grayson-perry-sarabande-foundation-lee-alexander-mcqueen-inspiration-series.

9 Hutton, "Artist Grayson Perry."

10 Perry, *Descent of Man*, 61.

11 Ian Kelly, *Beau Brummell: The Ultimate Man of Style* (New York: Simon & Schuster, 2006), 39.

12 Kelly, *Beau Brummell*, 60–61.

13 Kelly, *Beau Brummell*, 60–61.

14 Oscar Wilde, "The Philosophy of Dress," New York *Tribune*, April 19, 1885.

15 Richard Ellman, "Wilde in New York: Beauty Packed Them In," *New York Times*, November 1, 1987.

16 Frances Hodgson Burnett, *Little Lord Fauntleroy* (Scribner's, 1886; repr., Puffin, 2015), 71.

17 Gregory M. Pflugfelder, "The Nation-State, the Age/Gender System, and the Reconstitution of Erotic Desire in Nineteenth-Century Japan," *Journal of Asian Studies* 71, no. 4 (2012): 963–74, https://doi.org/10.1017/s0021911812001222.

18 Smithsonian Museums: National Museum of African American Culture and History.

19 "I Would Die 4 U," by Prince Rogers Nelson, June 25, 1984.

20 "Controversy," by Prince Rogers Nelson, October 14, 1981.

21 Robert Enright and Meeka Walsh, "Esmaa Mohamoud, Game Changer," *Border Crossings*, November 2020, https://bordercrossingsmag.com/article/esmaa-mohamoud.

22 Connor Garel, "Artist Esmaa Mohamoud Examines How Pro Sports Profit from Black Athletes," *The Walrus*, January 30, 2022, https://thewalrus.ca/loveofthegame-artist-esmaa-mohamoud-examines-how-pro-sports-profit-from-black-athletes/.

23 Amanda Parris, "Why Esmaa Mohamoud Is Bringing Blackness and Basketball into the Gallery," CBC, July 20, 2017, https://www.si.com/lifestyle/2019/07/22/athlete-fashion-pregame-arena-tunnel-entrance-photograph-nba-nfl-nhl-style.

24 Maya Singer, "When Sports Met Fashion," *Vogue*, Winter 2025, 81.

25 Linda M. Heywood, *Njinga of Angola: Africa's Warrior Queen* (Harvard University Press, 2019), 127.

26 Heywood, *Njinga of Angola*, 75–76.

27 Kevin Tervala, Matthew S. Polk Jr., and Amy L. Gould, *Kuba: Fabric of an Empire*, exh. cat. (Baltimore Museum of Art, 2018), 74–88.

28 Rachel Jones, "The True Story of the Women Warriors of Dahomey," *National Geographic News*, September 14, 2022.

29 Mike Dash, "Dahomey's Women Warriors," *Smithsonian*, September 23, 2011.

30 Frederick E. Forbes, *Dahomey and the Dahomans: Being the Journals of Two Missions to the King of Dahomey, and Residence at His Capital, in the Years 1849 and 1850*, vol. 1. (Longman, Brown, Green, and Longmans, 1851), 119, https://doi.org/10.5479/sil.257101.39088000286781.

31 "Hatshepsut in a Devotional Attitude" (Metropolitan Museum of Art, 2020), https://www.metmuseum.org/art/collection/search/544849.

32 "Hatshepsut in a Devotional Attitude."

33 "Hatshepsut in a Devotional Attitude."

34 Kit Heyam, *Before We Were Trans* (Seal Press, 2022), 42–43.

35 Catharine H. Roehrig, *Hatshepsut: From Queen to Pharaoh* (Yale University Press and Metropolitan Museum of Art, 2005), 9.

36 Queen Elizabeth I, "Tilbury Speech," August 9, 1588.

37 Kate Wilkinson, "Young, Female and Powerful: Was Elizabeth I a Feminist?" Royal Museums Greenwich, November 16, 2017, https://www.rmg.co.uk/stories/blog/young-female-powerful-was-elizabeth-i-feminist.

TRIAD

1 Heyam, *Before We Were Trans*, 61.

2 Heyam, *Before We Were Trans*, 73.

3 Heyam, *Before We Were Trans*, 218.

4 Laxmi Narayan Tripathi, *Me Hijra, Me Laxmi*, trans. Ramachandrapurapu Raj Rao and Padmakar G. Joshi (Oxford University Press, 2015), 122.

5 Dan Taulapapa McMullin, *The Healer's Wound, a Queer Theirstory of Polynesia* (Tropic Editions, 2022).

6 Queer Music Heritage, courtesy of J. D. Doyle, https://queermusicheritage.com/.

7 David Hudson, *Memoir of Jemima Wilkinson* (1821; repr., Underhill, 1844), 130-31.

8 Hudson, *Memoir of Jemima Wilkinson*, 144-45.

9 Herbert A. Wisbey, *Pioneer Prophetess: Jemima Wilkinson, the Publick Universal Friend* (Cornell University Press, 2018).

10 Frank Bird Linderman, *Red Mother* (John Day, 1932), reissued as *Pretty-shield: Medicine Woman of the Crows* (Bison Books, 1972), 228.

11 Linderman, *Pretty-shield*, 230.

12 Christian Allaire, "This Indigenous Two-Spirit Couple Matches Their Regalia," *Vogue*, August 17, 2020, https://www.vogue.com/article/adrian-matthias-stevens-and-sean-snyder-indigenous-two-spirit-couple.

13 Linderman, *Pretty-shield*, 233.

14 James Brust, in discussion with the author, June 18, 2024.

15 "A Zuni Princess: Interesting Facts Concerning a Strange People," *National Tribune*, May 20, 1886, https://www.loc.gov/item/sn82016187/1886-05-20/ed-1/.

16 Will Roscoe, "We'wha and Klah the American Indian Berdache as Artist and Priest," *American Indian Quarterly* 12, no. 2 (1988): 127, https://doi.org/10.2307/1184319.

17 "A Zuni Princess."

18 William MacDuff, "Beautiful Boys in Nō Drama: The Idealization of Homoerotic Desire," *Asian Theatre Journal* 13, no. 2 (Autumn 1996): 248–58, https://www.jstor.org/stable/1124529.

19 Stephen O. Murray and Will Roscoe, eds., *Boy-Wives and Female Husbands: Studies of African Homosexualities* (Palgrave Macmillan, 1998), 159–60.

20 Giovanni Antonio Cavazzi, "Missione Evangelica al Regno del Congo" (the Araldi manuscript), vol. C, MAVCOR (https://mavcor.yale.edu/material-objects/giovanni-antonio-cavazzi-missione-evangelica-al-regno-del-congo-araldi-manuscript).

21 James H. Sweet, *Recreating Africa Culture, Kinship, and Religion in the African-Portuguese World, 1441–1770* (University of North Carolina Press, 2003), 53.

22 James H. Sweet, "Mutual Misunderstandings: Gesture, Gender, and Healing in the African Portuguese World," *Past & Present* 203, no. 4 (2009): 133, https://doi.org/10.1093/pastj/gtp006.

AFTERWORD

1 Nicole Gnesa, email to the author, June 25, 2024.

2 Nadja Sayej, "Eva & Adele: When I See You My Heart Is Dancing," http://www.evaadele.com/texts/bpea.pdf.

3 Sayej, "Eva & Adele: When I See You My Heart Is Dancing."

4 Noah Khoshbin, in discussion with the author, July 9, 2024.

5 Richard Gallo, 1973, as quoted by Noah Khoshbin, in discussion with the author, July 9, 2024.

6 Hawes, *Fashion Is Spinach*, 291–311.

SELECT BIBLIOGRAPHY

Abrams Books. *Dress Like a Woman: Working Women and What They Wore.* Abrams, 2018.

Adie, Kate, with the Imperial War Museum. *Corsets to Camouflage: Women and War.* Hachette UK, 2004.

Allaire, Christian. *The Power of Style: How Fashion and Beauty Are Being Used to Reclaim Cultures.* Annick, 2021.

Arnold, Rebecca. *Fashion, Desire and Anxiety: Image and Morality in the Twentieth Century.* Rutgers University Press, 2001.

Backett-Milburn, K., and L. McKie. *Constructing Gendered Bodies.* Springer, 2001.

Banks, Jeffrey, and Doria de la Chapelle. *Tartan: Romancing the Plaid.* Rizzoli, 2015.

Barber, Elizabeth Wayland. *Women's Work: The First 20,000 Years.* W. W. Norton, 1995.

Barnes, Ruth, and Joanne B. Eicher. *Dress and Gender: Making and Meaning.* Berg, 1992.

Bendall, Sarah. *Shaping Femininity: Foundation Garments, the Body and Women in Early Modern England.* Bloomsbury, 2021.

Besnier, Niko, and Kalissa Alexeyeff. *Gender on the Edge: Transgender, Gay, and Other Pacific Islanders.* University of Hawai'i Press, 2014.

Blank, Hanne. *Straight: The Surprisingly Short History of Heterosexuality.* Beacon, 2012.

Bullough, Vern L., and Bonnie Bullough. *Cross Dressing, Sex, and Gender.* University of Pennsylvania Press, 1993.

Burrows, Simon, Jonathan Conlin, Russell Goulbourne, and Valerie Mainz. *The Chevalier d'Éon and His Worlds: Gender, Espionage and Politics in the Eighteenth Century.* A & C Black, 2011.

Butler, Judith. *Who's Afraid of Gender?* Knopf Canada, 2024.

Cage, E. Claire. "The Sartorial Self: Neoclassical Fashion and Gender Identity in France, 1797–1804." *Eighteenth-Century Studies* 42, no. 2 (Winter 2009): 193–215. https://www.jstor.org/stable/40264250.

Cavallaro, Dani, and Alexandra Warwick. *Fashioning the Frame: Boundaries, Dress and the Body.* Berg, 1998.

Chapin, Chloe. "Masculine Renunciation or Rejection of the Feminine?: Revisiting J. C. Flügel's *Psychology of Clothes.*" *Fashion Theory* 26, no. 7 (October 11, 2021): 983–1008. https://doi.org/10.1080/1362704x.2021.1952919.

Cifarelli, Megan. *Fashioned Selves: Dress and Identity in Antiquity.* Oxbow, 2019.

Cole, Shaun. *Don We Now Our Gay Apparel: Gay Men's Dress in the Twentieth Century.* Berg, 2000.

Cook, Matt, Robert Mills, Randolph Trumbach, and H. G. Cocks. *A Gay History of Britain: Love and Sex Between Men Since the Middle Ages.* Praeger, 2007.

Crane, Diana. *Fashion and Its Social Agendas: Class, Gender, and Identity in Clothing.* University of Chicago Press, 2000.

Cumming, Valerie. *A Visual History of Costume: The Sixteenth Century.* Quite Specific Media, 1983.

Dawson, Tracy. *Let Me Be Frank: A Book About Women Who Dressed Like Men to Do Shit They Weren't Supposed to Do.* HarperCollins, 2022.

Deitcher, David. *Dear Friends: American Photographs of Men Together, 1840–1918.* Abrams, 2001.

de la Haye, Amy, and Elizabeth Wilson. *Defining Dress: Dress as Object, Meaning, and Identity.* Manchester University Press, 1999.

Delpierre, Madeleine. *Dress in France in the Eighteenth Century.* Yale University Press, 1997.

Faderman, Lillian. *Surpassing the Love of Men: Romantic Friendship and Love Between Women from the Renaissance to the Present.* William Morrow, 1985.

Fausto-Sterling, Anne. *Sexing the Body: Gender Politics and the Construction of Sexuality.* Basic Books, 2020.

Fisher, Will. *Materializing Gender in Early Modern English Literature and Culture.* Cambridge University Press, 2006.

Flügel, John Carl. *The Psychology of Clothes.* Hogarth, 1971.

Ford, Elyssa. *Rodeo as Refuge, Rodeo as Rebellion: Gender, Race, and Identity in the American Rodeo.* University Press of Kansas, 2020.

Ford, Richard Thompson. *Dress Codes: How the Laws of Fashion Made History.* Simon & Schuster, 2022.

Fréger, Charles. *Wilder Mann: The Image of the Savage.* Dewi Lewis Publishing, 2012.

Fréger, Charles. *Yokainoshima: Island of Monsters.* Thames & Hudson, 2016.

Friedman, David M. *Wilde in America: Oscar Wilde and the Invention of Modern Celebrity.* W. W. Norton, 2014.

Fussell, Paul. *Uniforms: Why We Are What We Wear.* Houghton Mifflin Harcourt, 2002.

Geczy, Adam, and Vicki Karaminas. *Queer Style.* Bloomsbury, 2013.

Griggs, Claudine. *S/he: Changing Sex and Changing Clothes*. Berg, 1998.

Hawes, Elizabeth. *Fashion Is Spinach*. Random House, 1938.

Hawes, Elizabeth. *Why Is a Dress?: Who? What? When? Where?* Viking, 1942.

Heyam, Kit. *Before We Were Trans: A New History of Gender*. Seal, 2022.

Hollander, Anne. *Sex and Suits: The Evolution of Modern Dress*. Bloomsbury, 2016.

Jones, Jennifer. *Sexing La Mode: Gender, Fashion and Commercial Culture in Old Regime France*. Berg, 2004.

Jones, Kevin L., and Christina M. Johnson. *Sporting Fashion: Outdoor Girls 1800 to 1960*. National Geographic Books, 2021.

Kaplan, Joel H., and Sheila Stowell. *Theatre and Fashion: Oscar Wilde to the Suffragettes*. Cambridge University Press, 1994.

Karaminas, Vicki, Adam Geczy, and Pamela Church Gibson. *Fashionable Masculinities: Queers, Pimp Daddies, and Lumbersexuals*. Rutgers University Press, 2022.

Kidwell, Claudia Brush, and Margaret C. S. Christman. *Suiting Everyone: The Democratization of Clothing in America*. Smithsonian Institution Press, 1974.

Kidwell, Claudia Brush, and Valerie Steele. *Men and Women: Dressing the Part*. Smithsonian Books, 1989.

Laxmi, R. Raj Rao, and P. G. Joshi. *Me Hijra, Me Laxmi*. Oxford University Press, 2015.

Linderman, Frank Bird. *Pretty-shield: Medicine Woman of the Crows*. Bison, 1972.

Lynch, Annette. *Dress, Gender and Cultural Change: Asian American and African American Rites of Passage*. Berg, 1999.

Mackinney-Valentin, Maria. *Fashioning Identity: Status Ambivalence in Contemporary Fashion*. Bloomsbury, 2017.

Mauriès, Patrick. *Androgyne: Fashion and Gender*. National Geographic Books, 2017.

McBride, Richard D. "Silla Buddhism and the *Hwarang*." *Korean Studies* 34, no. 1 (2010): 54–89. https://doi.org/10.1353/ks.2008.0007.

McMullin, Dan Taulapapa. *Coconut Milk*. University of Arizona Press, 2013.

McNeil, Peter. "'That Doubtful Gender': Macaroni Dress and Male Sexualities." *Fashion Theory* 3, no. 4 (November 1999): 411–47. https://doi.org/10.2752/136270499779476081.

Monden, Masafumi. *Japanese Fashion Cultures: Dress and Gender in Contemporary Japan*. Bloomsbury, 2014.

Moore, Madison. *Fabulous: The Rise of the Beautiful Eccentric*. Yale University Press, 2018.

Mostow, Joshua S., Asato Ikeda, and Ryoko Matsuba. *A Third Gender: Beautiful Youths in Japanese Edo-Period Prints and Paintings (1600–1868)*. Hotei, 2016.

Paoletti, Jo B. *Pink and Blue: Telling the Boys from the Girls in America*. Indiana University Press, 2012.

Paoletti, Jo B. *Sex and Unisex: Fashion, Feminism, and the Sexual Revolution*. Indiana University Press, 2015.

Perry, Grayson. *The Descent of Man*. Penguin, 2017.

Perry, Grayson, Victoria Coren Mitchell, Patrick Elliott, and Tor Scott. *Grayson Perry: Smash Hits*. National Galleries of Scotland, 2023.

Piponnier, Françoise, and Perrine Mane. *Dress in the Middle Ages*. Yale University Press, 1997.

Purks Maccubbin, Robert. *'Tis Nature's Fault: Unauthorized Sexuality during the Enlightenment*. Cambridge University Press, 1987.

Pyun, Kyunghee, and Minjee Kim, eds. *Dress History of Korea: Critical Perspectives on Primary Sources*. Bloomsbury, 2023.

Reilly, Andrew, and Ben Barry. *Crossing Gender Boundaries: Fashion to Create, Disrupt and Transcend*. Intellect, 2020.

Reynolds, Simon. *Shock and Awe: Glam Rock and Its Legacy, from the Seventies to the Twenty-First Century*. HarperCollins, 2016.

Roach-Higgins, Mary Ellen, Joanne Bubolz Eicher, and Kim K. P. Johnson. *Dress and Identity*. Fairchild, 1995.

Robertson, Jennifer. "The Politics of Androgyny in Japan: Sexuality and Subversion in the Theater and Beyond." *American Ethnologist* 19, no. 3 (August 1992): 419–42. https://doi.org/10.1525/ae.1992.19.3.02a00010.

Senelick, Laurence. *The Changing Room: Sex, Drag and Theatre*. Routledge, 2002.

Shen, Lisa Chu. "Gender and Cross-Genderism in Children's Literature: A Comparative Case Study of the Figure of the Tomboy." *Neohelicon* 45, no. 2 (June 12, 2018): 653–70. https://doi.org/10.1007/s11059-018-0436-y.

Smith, Catherine, and Cynthia Greig. *Women in Pants: Manly Maidens, Cowgirls, and Other Renegades*. Harry N. Abrams, 2003.

Smith, Kiki. *Real Clothes, Real Lives: 200 Years of What Women Wore*. Rizzoli, 2023.

Steele, Valerie. *The Corset: A Cultural History*. Yale University Press, 2001.

Strassfeld, Max K. *Trans Talmud: Androgynes and Eunuchs in Rabbinic Literature*. University of California Press, 2023.

Suthrell, Charlotte. *Unzipping Gender: Sex, Cross-Dressing and Culture*. Berg, 2004.

Trevor-Roper, Hugh. *The Invention of Scotland*. Yale University Press, 2008.

Veblen, Thorstein. *The Theory of the Leisure Class*. Routledge, 2017.

Waine, Rosie. *Highland Style: Fashioning Highland Dress, c. 1745–1845*. National Museums Scotland, 2022.

Wild, Benjamin Linley. *Carnival to Catwalk: Global Reflections on Fancy Dress Costume*. Bloomsbury, 2020.

Wisbey, Herbert A. *Pioneer Prophetess: Jemima Wilkinson, the Publick Universal Friend*. Cornell University Press, 2018.

Woodard, Jennie. "Skirts for Men!: Elizabeth Hawes and Challenging Fashion's Gender Binary." *Journal of Popular Culture* 50, no. 6 (December 17, 2017): 1276–92. https://doi.org/10.1111/jpcu.12628.

Woolf, Virginia. *Orlando: A Biography*. Hogarth Press, 1928.

IMAGE CREDITS

11: Qween Jean, photo: Ryan McGinley, courtesy of *American Theatre* magazine (published by Theatre Communications Group)

12: Courtesy of Michael Sylvan Robinson, photo: Paul Takeuchi, 2024

14 (left): Courtesy of Michael Sylvan Robinson, photo: Jenna Bascom, 2021; (right): Courtesy of Michael Sylvan Robinson, photo: Paul Takeuchi, 2024

16: © Charles Freger, 059

17: © Charles Freger, 058

20: Photo: Takahashi Munemasa, https://www.diversity-in-the-arts.jp/

23: The Chung Young Yang Embroidery Museum

24: © 2024 Urbody Functional Fashion, photo: Nicholas Caiazza

27: © Beefcake Swimwear 2024, photo: Adrianna Reid

28: ZUMA Press, Inc. / Alamy Stock Photo

30: @NOWFashion

31: @NOWFashion

32: © Daniele Trese

34: © NOWFashion

35 (left): © NOWFashion; (right): © NOWFashion

36: © Gwyn Conaway, 2024

38: © Kelly Ruiz

39: Gift of Mr. and Mrs. Carter H. Harrison, Art Institute of Chicago

41: Gift of Mrs. John Knapp Hollins, in memory of her husband, 1959, the Metropolitan Museum of Art

42: Orlando (Tilda Swinton) in the film *Orlando*, courtesy of Sally Potter, photo: Liam Longman © Adventure Pictures Ltd

45: @ Gwyn Conaway, 2024

46: The Prop Gallery, UK, 2024

47: © Gwyn Conaway, 2024

48: Free Library of Philadelphia, Philadelphia, United States, John Frederick Lewis Collection of European Manuscripts

49: The Picture Art Collection / Alamy Stock Photo

50: Andrew W. Mellon Collection, National Art Gallery, public domain

52 (top): Jon Arnold Images Ltd / Alamy Stock Photo; (bottom): Olivier Adam

56: Patons UK, 1970 knitting pattern, courtesy of Rowan & Patons, DMC, 2025

59: © Gwyn Conaway, 2024

61: London (Florence House, Barnes, London S.W.): Inter-Art Co. [between 1920 and 1929], courtesy of the Wellcome Collection, part of the James Gardiner Collection, reference: 2059303i

62: Courtesy of the Estate of Patricia Faure, thanks to Zazu Faure, Rudi Gernreich papers, UCLA Library Special Collections

63: "Thayaht in TuTa," Florence, 1920, courtesy of the Thayaht & RAM Archive, Florence, Italy, photo: Pietro Salvini—Firenze

64 (top): "Tuttintuta," Florence, 1920, courtesy of the Thayaht & RAM Archive, Florence, Italy; (bottom left): "How to Cut the TuTa," courtesy of the Thayaht & RAM Archive, Florence, Italy; (bottom right): "The Female TuTa," courtesy of the Galleria del Costume, n. inv. 7591, Palazzo Pitti, Firenze, Italy

65: Penta Springs Limited / Alamy Stock Photo

67 (top left): Harvard University—Boston Museum of Fine Arts Expedition; (top right): Wikimedia Commons, public domain; (bottom): The Metropolitan Museum of Art

72: FIDM Museum Purchase, ASU FIDM Museum Collection

74: © Troy Morgan

75: © Troy Morgan

76–77: © Troy Morgan

78 (top and bottom): © Paramount Pictures Corporation

80: BFA / Alamy Stock Photo

81: Lilli Wolff (designer) and Mati Driessen (dressmaker), Maifest debutante dress sketch, 1958, gift of Carolyn Williams, Texas Fashion Collection, University of North Texas College of Visual Arts and Design, Denton, Texas

82: Lilli Wolff (designer) and Mati Driessen (dressmaker), Maifest debutante dress, 1958, gift of Carolyn Williams, Texas Fashion Collection, University of North Texas College of Visual Arts and Design, Denton, Texas

83: Photograph of Maifest in Brenham, Texas, 1958, gift of Harriet Peavy, Texas Fashion Collection, University of North Texas College of Visual Arts and Design, Denton, Texas

84: © Shawshots / Alamy Stock Photo

86: © Gwyn Conaway, 2024

87: © Gwyn Conaway, 2024

88: Rick Rudnicki / Alamy Stock Photo

89: Trinity Mirror / Mirrorpix / Alamy Stock Photo

90: Archives Center Lesbian, Gay, Bisexual, Transgender (LGBT) Collection, Archives Center, National Museum of American History, Smithsonian Institution

92: thislife pictures / Alamy Stock Photo and Palczewski, Catherine H. Postcard Archive, University of Northern Iowa, Cedar Falls, Iowa

95: The Print Collector / Alamy Stock Photo